# vegetarian

# introduction

Following a vegetarian diet was once considered to be rather eccentric and certainly very dull! However, in recent years more and more people have chosen to embrace a meat-free diet, for a number of reasons. The most obvious of these is a desire not to eat animals or fish, but health issues often come into the equation too – for example, sufferers of irritable bowel syndrome often find that meat is one of the triggers for the symptoms. Meat and fish can also be expensive, so even non-vegetarians often choose to have two or three meat-free meals each week.

The really good news is that the ever-increasing interest in vegetarianism has raised its profile in the world of gastronomy. Chefs have risen to the challenge with skill and enthusiasm and have come up with some truly creative recipes – and the meat-free diet is no longer dull!

If you are new to vegetarianism, it is important to remember that you cannot simply exclude meat and fish from your usual recipes, because this will deprive you of protein and other vital nutrients that are essential to your health and wellbeing. Meat and fish must be replaced with other protein- and nutrient-rich foods such as beans, nuts and seeds, tofu and dairy products. If you have allergies to any of these foods, take advice from your doctor or a nutritionist to ensure that you will not damage your health instead of enhancing it.

Whether you are planning to be a 'proper' vegetarian, or you are having vegetarian guests to dinner, or you just want to ring the changes and have an occasional meal without meat, there are some fabulous ideas in this book, taken from around the world. For the best results, choose really fresh, top-quality ingredients – this will ensure that you get the maximum goodness out of your food, as well as superb flavour.

Have fun experimenting!

# light meals & starters

# cracked marinated olives

## ingredients

### serves 8

450 g/1 lb can or jar unpitted large
    green olives, drained
4 garlic cloves, peeled
2 tsp coriander seeds
1 small lemon
4 sprigs of fresh thyme
4 feathery stalks of fennel
2 small fresh red chillies (optional)
pepper
Spanish extra-virgin olive oil,
    to cover
slices of fresh crusty bread,
    to serve

## method

1 To allow the flavours of the marinade to penetrate the olives, place the olives on a cutting board and, using a rolling pin, bash them lightly so that they crack slightly. Alternatively, use a sharp knife to cut a lengthways slit in each olive as far as the stone. Using the flat side of a broad knife, lightly crush each garlic clove. Using a pestle and mortar, crack the coriander seeds. Cut the lemon, with its rind, into small chunks.

2 Put the olives, garlic, coriander seeds, lemon chunks, thyme sprigs, fennel and chillies, if using, in a large bowl and toss together. Season with pepper, but you should not need to add salt as preserved olives are usually salty enough. Pack the ingredients tightly into a glass jar with a lid. Pour in enough olive oil to cover the olives, then seal the jar tightly.

3 Let the olives stand at room temperature for 24 hours, then marinate in the refrigerator for at least 1 week but preferably 2 weeks before serving. From time to time, gently give the jar a shake to remix the ingredients. Return the olives to room temperature and remove from the oil to serve. Provide cocktail sticks for spearing the olives. Serve with slices of fresh crusty bread.

# salted almonds

## ingredients

### serves 6–8

225 g/8 oz whole almonds, in their skins or blanched (see method)
4 tbsp Spanish olive oil
coarse sea salt
1 tsp paprika or ground cumin (optional)

## method

1 Fresh almonds in their skins are superior in taste, but blanched almonds are much more convenient. If the almonds are not blanched, put them in a bowl, cover with boiling water for 3–4 minutes, then plunge them into cold water for 1 minute. Drain them well in a sieve, then slide off the skins between your fingers. Dry the almonds well on kitchen paper.

2 Put the olive oil in a roasting pan and swirl it round so that it covers the bottom. Add the almonds and toss them in the pan so that they are evenly coated in the oil, then spread them out in a single layer.

3 Roast the almonds in a preheated oven, 180°C/350°F/ Gas Mark 4, for 20 minutes, or until they are light golden brown, tossing several times during the cooking. Drain the almonds on kitchen paper, then transfer them to a bowl.

4 While the almonds are still warm, sprinkle with plenty of sea salt and the paprika or cumin, if using, and toss well together to coat. Serve the almonds warm or cold. The almonds are at their best when served freshly cooked, so, if possible, cook them on the day that you plan to eat them. However, they can be stored in an airtight container for up to 3 days.

# hummus

## ingredients

### serves 8

225 g/8 oz dried chickpeas,
    covered with water and
    soaked overnight
juice of 2 large lemons
150 ml/5 fl oz tahini
2 garlic cloves, crushed
4 tbsp extra-virgin olive oil
small pinch of ground cumin
salt and pepper
1 tsp paprika
chopped flat-leaf parsley,
    to garnish
pitta bread, to serve

## method

*1* Drain the chickpeas, put in a saucepan, and cover with cold water. Bring to the boil then let simmer for about 2 hours, until very tender.

*2* Drain the chickpeas, reserving a little of the liquid, and put in a food processor, reserving a few to garnish. Blend the chickpeas until smooth, gradually adding the lemon juice and enough reserved liquid to form a smooth, thick purée.

*3* Add the tahini, garlic, 3 tablespoons of the olive oil and the cumin and blend until smooth. Season with salt and pepper.

*4* Turn the mixture into a shallow serving dish and chill in the refrigerator for 2–3 hours before serving.

*5* To serve, mix the reserved olive oil with the paprika and drizzle over the top of the dish. Sprinkle with the parsley and the reserved chickpeas. Accompany with warm pitta bread.

# guacamole

## ingredients

*serves 4*

2 large, ripe avocados
juice of 1 lime, or to taste
2 tsp olive oil
½ onion, finely chopped
1 fresh green chilli, such as
    poblano, deseeded and finely
    chopped
1 garlic clove, crushed
¼ tsp ground cumin
1 tbsp chopped fresh coriander,
    plus extra leaves to garnish
    (optional)
salt and pepper

## method

1 Cut the avocados in half lengthways and twist the 2 halves in opposite directions to separate. Stab the stone with the point of a sharp knife and lift out.

2 Peel, then coarsely chop, the avocado halves and place in a non-metallic bowl. Squeeze over the lime juice and add the oil.

3 Mash the avocados with a fork until the desired consistency is reached – either chunky or smooth. Blend in the onion, chilli, garlic, cumin and chopped coriander, then season with salt and pepper.

4 Transfer to a serving dish and serve at once, to avoid discoloration, garnished with the coriander leaves, if liked.

# aubergine pâté

## ingredients

*serves 4–6*

2 large aubergines
4 tbsp extra virgin olive oil
2 garlic cloves, very finely chopped
4 tbsp lemon juice
salt and pepper
6 crisp breads, to serve

## method

1 Score the skins of the aubergines with the point of a sharp knife, without piercing the flesh, and place them on a baking sheet. Bake in a preheated oven, 180°C/350°F/Gas Mark 4, for 1¼ hours, or until soft.

2 Remove the aubergines from the oven and leave until cool enough to handle. Cut them in half and, using a spoon, scoop out the flesh into a bowl. Mash the flesh thoroughly.

3 Gradually beat in the olive oil then stir in the garlic and lemon juice. Season to taste with salt and pepper. Cover with clingfilm and store in the refrigerator until required. Serve with the crisp breads.

# borscht

## ingredients

### serves 6

1 onion
55 g/2 oz butter
350 g/12 oz raw beetroot, cut into thin batons, and 1 raw beetroot, grated
1 carrot, cut into thin batons
3 celery sticks, thinly sliced
2 tomatoes, peeled, deseeded and chopped
1.4 litres/2½ pints vegetable stock
1 tbsp white wine vinegar
1 tbsp sugar
2 large fresh dill sprigs
115 g/4 oz white cabbage, shredded
salt and pepper
150 ml/5 fl oz soured cream, to garnish

## method

**1** Slice the onion into rings. Melt the butter in a large, heavy-based saucepan. Add the onion and cook over a low heat, stirring occasionally, for 3–5 minutes, or until softened. Add the beetroot batons, carrot, celery and chopped tomatoes and cook, stirring frequently, for 4–5 minutes.

**2** Add the stock, vinegar and sugar, and snip a tablespoon of dill into the saucepan. Season to taste with salt and pepper. Bring to the boil, reduce the heat and simmer for 35–40 minutes, or until the vegetables are tender.

**3** Stir in the cabbage, cover and simmer for 10 minutes. Stir in the grated beetroot, with any juices, and cook for a further 10 minutes. Ladle into warmed bowls. Garnish with a spoonful of soured cream and another tablespoon of snipped dill and serve.

# vegetable soup with pesto

## ingredients

### serves 4

1 litre/32 fl oz fresh cold water
bouquet garni of 1 fresh parsley
    sprig, 1 fresh thyme sprig, and
    1 bay leaf, tied together with
    clean string
2 celery stalks, chopped
3 baby leeks, chopped
4 baby carrots, chopped
150 g/5½ oz new potatoes,
    scrubbed and cut into bite-size
    chunks
4 tbsp shelled broad beans or peas
175 g/6 oz canned cannellini
    or flageolet beans, drained
    and rinsed
3 heads pak choi
150 g/5½ oz rocket
pepper

### pesto

2 large handfuls fresh basil leaves
1 fresh green chilli, deseeded
2 garlic cloves
4 tbsp olive oil
1 tsp Parmesan cheese,
    finely grated

## method

1 Put the water and bouquet garni into a large saucepan
and add the celery, leeks, carrots and potatoes. Bring to
the boil, then reduce the heat and simmer for 10 minutes.

2 Stir in the broad beans or peas and canned beans and
simmer for a further 10 minutes. Stir in the pak choi and
rocket, season with pepper and simmer for a further
2–3 minutes. Remove and discard the bouquet garni.

3 Meanwhile, to make the pesto, put the basil, chilli,
garlic and oil into a food processor and pulse to form
a thick paste. Stir in the cheese.

4 Stir most of the pesto into the soup, then ladle into
warmed bowls. Top with the remaining pesto and
serve at once.

# watercress soup

## ingredients

### serves 4

2 bunches of watercress (approx 200 g/7 oz), thoroughly cleaned
3 tbsp butter
2 onions, chopped
225 g/8 oz potatoes, peeled and roughly chopped
1.25 litres/40 fl oz vegetable stock or water
salt and pepper
whole nutmeg, for grating (optional)
125 ml/4 fl oz crème fraîche, yogurt, or sour cream

## method

1 Remove the leaves from the stalks of the watercress and keep on one side. Roughly chop the stalks.

2 Melt the butter in a large saucepan over medium heat, add the onion and cook for 4–5 minutes until soft. Do not brown.

3 Add the potato to the pan and mix well with the onion. Add the watercress stalks and the stock. Bring to the boil, then reduce the heat, cover and simmer for 15–20 minutes until the potato is soft.

4 Add the watercress leaves and stir in to heat through. Remove from the heat and use a hand-held stick blender to process the soup until smooth. Alternatively, pour the soup into a blender, process until smooth, and return to the rinsed-out pan. Reheat and season with salt and pepper, adding a good grating of nutmeg, if using.

5 Serve in warm bowls with the crème fraîche, yogurt or sour cream spooned on top.

# white bean soup

## ingredients

### serves 4

175 g/6 oz dried cannellini beans,
    soaked in cold water to cover
    overnight
1.5 litres/48 fl oz vegetable stock
115 g/4 oz dried corallini,
    conchigliette piccole,
    or other soup pasta
6 tbsp olive oil
2 garlic cloves, finely chopped
4 tbsp chopped fresh
    flat-leaf parsley
salt and pepper
fresh crusty bread, to serve

## method

1 Drain the soaked beans and place them in a large,
    heavy-based saucepan. Add the stock and bring to the
    boil. Partially cover the pan, then reduce the heat and
    simmer for 2 hours, or until tender.

2 Transfer about half the beans and a little of the stock to
    a food processor or blender and process to a smooth
    purée. Return the purée to the pan and stir well to mix.
    Return the soup to the boil.

3 Add the pasta to the soup, return to the boil and cook
    for 10 minutes, or until tender.

4 Meanwhile, heat 4 tablespoons of the olive oil in
    a small saucepan. Add the garlic and cook over low
    heat, stirring frequently, for 4–5 minutes, or until
    golden. Stir the garlic into the soup and add the
    parsley. Season with salt and pepper and ladle into
    warmed soup bowls. Drizzle with the remaining olive
    oil and serve immediately with crusty bread.

# chinese mushroom soup

## ingredients

### serves 4

15 g/½ oz dried Chinese wood ear
    mushrooms
115 g/4 oz dried thin Chinese egg
    noodles
2 tsp arrowroot or cornstarch
1 litre/32 fl oz vegetable stock
5-cm/2-inch piece fresh ginger,
    peeled and sliced
2 tbsp dark soy sauce
2 tsp mirin or sweet sherry
1 tsp rice vinegar
4 small pak choi, each cut in half
salt and pepper
snipped fresh Chinese or ordinary
    chives, to garnish

## method

1 Put the dried wood ear mushrooms in a heatproof
bowl and pour over enough boiling water to cover,
then let stand for 20 minutes, or until tender.
Meanwhile, boil the noodles for 3 minutes, or according
to the package instructions, until soft. Drain well and
rinse with cold water to stop the noodles cooking,
and set aside.

2 Strain the mushrooms through a sieve lined with a dish
towel and reserve the liquid. Leave the mushrooms
whole or slice them, depending on how large they are.
Put the arrowroot in a wok or large pan and gradually
stir in the reserved mushroom liquid. Add the
vegetable stock, sliced ginger, soy sauce, mirin, rice
vinegar, mushrooms and pak choi and bring to the
boil, stirring constantly. Lower the heat and simmer
for 15 minutes.

3 Add salt and pepper, but remember that soy sauce is
salty so you might not need any salt at all – taste first.
Use a slotted spoon to remove the pieces of ginger.

4 Divide the noodles between 4 bowls, then spoon the
soup over and garnish with chives.

# tomato bruschetta

## ingredients

*serves 4*

8 slices of rustic bread
4 garlic cloves, halved
8 plum tomatoes, peeled and diced
extra virgin olive oil, for drizzling
salt and pepper
fresh basil leaves, to garnish

## method

1 Preheat the grill. Lightly toast the bread on both sides.
Rub each piece of toast with half a garlic clove and
then return to the grill for a few seconds.

2 Divide the diced tomatoes among the toasts. Season
to taste with salt and pepper and drizzle with olive oil.
Serve immediately, garnished with basil leaves.

# mixed salad selection

## ingredients

*serves 4–6*

**celeriac rémoulade**

1 large egg yolk
1 tbsp Dijon mustard
$\frac{1}{2}$ tsp red wine vinegar
150 ml/5 fl oz sunflower oil
salt and pepper
1$\frac{1}{2}$ tsp lemon juice
1 tsp salt
450 g/1 lb celeriac

**carrot salad**

450 g/1 lb carrots, peeled
2 tbsp olive oil
2 tbsp freshly squeezed
    orange juice
salt and pepper
2 tbsp finely chopped almonds
1 tbsp finely chopped fresh
    flat-leaf parsley

**beetroot salad**

400 g/14 oz cooked
    beetroot, peeled
2 tbsp vinaigrette
1 tbsp snipped fresh chives
slices of French bread and
    unsalted butter, to serve

## method

1 To make the rémoulade sauce, whiz the egg yolk, mustard and red wine vinegar in a food processor or blender until blended. With the motor still running, pour the oil through the feed tube, drop by drop, until the sauce starts to thicken, then add the remainder of the oil in a slow, steady stream. Season to taste with salt and pepper.

2 Put the lemon juice and salt in a large bowl of water. Finely shred the celeriac into the acidulated water to prevent discoloration. Drain and pat dry, then stir into the rémoulade sauce. Let stand for 20 minutes at room temperature before serving.

3 To make the carrot salad, finely shred the carrots into a bowl with the olive oil and orange juice and toss together. Season with salt and pepper and cover and chill until required. Stir in the almonds and parsley just before serving.

4 To make the beetroot salad, cut the beetroot into 5-mm/$\frac{1}{4}$-inch dice. Put the diced beetroot in a bowl, then add the vinaigrette and toss together. Cover and chill until required. Stir in the chives just before serving.

5 To serve, divide the celeriac rémoulade, carrot salad and beetroot salad between individual plates and accompany with plenty of French bread and butter.

# figs with blue cheese

## ingredients

*serves 6*

**caramelized almonds**
100 g/3½ oz caster sugar
115 g/4 oz whole almonds,
　　blanched or unblanched

12 ripe figs
350 g/12 oz Spanish blue cheese,
　　such as Picós, crumbled
extra-virgin olive oil

## method

1 First make the caramelized almonds. Put the sugar in a saucepan over medium–high heat and stir until the sugar melts, turns golden brown and bubbles: do not stir once the mixture starts to bubble. Remove from the heat and add the almonds one at a time and quickly turn with a fork until coated; if the caramel hardens, return the pan to the heat. Transfer each almond to a lightly buttered baking sheet once it is coated. Let stand until cool and firm.

2 To serve, slice the figs in half and arrange 4 halves on each plate. Coarsely chop the almonds by hand, reserving a few whole ones for garnish. Place a mound of blue cheese on each plate and sprinkle with chopped almonds. Drizzle the figs very lightly with the oil and garnish with the reserved, whole almonds.

## variation

Try replacing the figs with pears for a tasty alternative.

# sautéed garlic mushrooms

## ingredients

*serves 6*

450 g/1 lb white mushrooms
5 tbsp Spanish olive oil
2 garlic cloves, finely chopped
squeeze of lemon juice
salt and pepper
4 tbsp chopped fresh
    flat-leaf parsley
crusty bread, to serve

## method

1 Wipe or brush clean the mushrooms, then trim off the stalks close to the caps. Cut any large mushrooms in half or into quarters. Heat the olive oil in a large, heavy-based frying pan, add the garlic and cook for 30 seconds–1 minute, or until lightly browned. Add the mushrooms and sauté over high heat, stirring most of the time, until the mushrooms have absorbed all the oil in the pan.

2 Reduce the heat to low. When the juices have come out of the mushrooms, increase the heat again, and sauté for 4–5 minutes, stirring most of the time, until the juices have almost evaporated. Add a squeeze of lemon juice and season to taste with salt and pepper. Stir in the chopped parsley and cook for a further minute.

3 Transfer the sautéed mushrooms to a warmed serving dish and serve piping hot or warm. Accompany with chunks or slices of crusty bread for mopping up the garlic cooking juices.

# courgette fritters with yogurt dip

## ingredients

### serves 4

2–3 courgettes, about
    400 g/14 oz
1 garlic clove, crushed
3 spring onions, finely sliced
125 g/4½ oz feta cheese,
    crumbled
2 tbsp finely chopped
    fresh parsley
2 tbsp finely chopped fresh mint
1 tbsp finely chopped fresh dill
½ tsp freshly grated nutmeg
2 tbsp all-purpose flour
pepper
2 eggs
2 tbsp olive oil
1 lemon, cut into quarters,
    to garnish

### yogurt dip

250 g/9 oz strained plain yogurt
¼ cucumber, diced
1 tbsp finely chopped fresh dill
pepper

## method

**1** Grate the courgettes straight onto a clean tea towel and cover with another. Pat well and set aside for 10 minutes until the courgettes are dry.

**2** Meanwhile, to make the dip, mix the yogurt, cucumber, dill and pepper in a serving bowl. Cover and chill.

**3** Tip the courgettes into a large mixing bowl. Stir in the garlic, spring onions, cheese, herbs, nutmeg, flour and pepper. Beat the eggs in a separate bowl and stir into the courgette mixture – the batter will be quite lumpy and uneven but this is fine.

**4** Heat the oil in a large, wide frying pan over medium heat. Drop 4 tablespoonfuls of the batter into the pan, with space in between, and cook for 2–3 minutes on each side. Remove, drain on kitchen paper and keep warm. Cook the second batch of fritters in the same way. (There should be 8 fritters in total.)

**5** Serve the fritters hot with the dip, garnished with lemon quarters.

# stuffed aubergine slices

## ingredients

*serves 4*

1 medium aubergine
4 tbsp extra virgin olive oil
115 g/4 oz mozzarella cheese,
   grated
1 tbsp fresh chopped basil
400 g/14 oz canned tomatoes with
   added herbs, heated through
extra basil leaves, to garnish

## method

1 Slice the aubergine lengthways into 8 slices. Brush the slices with oil and place on an ovenproof tray. Bake in a preheated oven, 200°C/400°F/Gas Mark 6, for 10 minutes, without letting them get too floppy. Remove from the oven. Scatter the grated cheese and basil over the aubergine slices.

2 Roll up each slice and place the slices in a single layer in a shallow ovenproof dish. Pour over the chopped tomatoes and bake in the oven for 10 minutes or until the sauce bubbles and the cheese melts.

3 Remove the stuffed aubergine slices from the oven and transfer carefully to serving plates. Spoon any remaining chopped tomatoes on or around the aubergine slices. Garnish with basil leaves and serve while still hot.

# asparagus with melted butter

## ingredients

### serves 2

16–20 stalks of asparagus, trimmed to about 20 cm/8 inches
85 g/3 oz unsalted butter, melted
sea salt and pepper, to serve

## method

1 Remove some of the base of the asparagus stalks with a potato peeler if they are rather thick. Tie the stalks together with string or use a wire basket so that they can easily be removed from the saucepan without damage.

2 Bring a large saucepan of salted water to the boil and plunge in the stalks. Cover with a lid and cook for 4–5 minutes. Pierce one stalk near the base with a sharp knife. If it is fairly soft remove from the heat at once. Do not overcook asparagus or the tender tips will fall off.

3 Drain the asparagus thoroughly and serve on large warmed plates with the butter poured over. Both the butter and the asparagus should be warm rather than hot. Serve with sea salt and pepper for sprinkling.

# vegetable tartlets

## ingredients

### makes 12

butter, for greasing
12 ready-baked puff pastry cases
2 tbsp olive oil
1 red pepper, deseeded
    and diced
1 garlic clove, crushed
1 small onion,
    finely chopped
225 g/8 oz ripe tomatoes, chopped
1 tbsp torn fresh basil
1 tsp fresh or dried thyme
salt and pepper
green salad, to serve

## method

1 Grease several baking trays. Place the ready-baked pastry cases on the prepared baking trays.

2 Heat the oil in a frying pan, add the pepper, garlic and onion and cook over a high heat for about 3 minutes until soft.

3 Add the tomatoes, herbs and seasoning and spoon onto the pastry cases.

4 Bake in a preheated oven, 200°C/400°F/Gas Mark 6, for about 5 minutes, or until the filling is piping hot. Serve warm with a green salad.

# cheese & herb soufflés with sautéed mushrooms

## ingredients

### serves 6

55 g/2 oz butter, plus extra,
    melted, for greasing
40 g/1½ oz all-purpose flour
150 ml/5 fl oz milk
250 g/9 oz ricotta cheese
4 eggs, separated, plus 2 egg
    whites
2 tbsp finely chopped fresh parsley
2 tbsp finely chopped fresh thyme
1 tbsp finely chopped fresh
    rosemary
salt and pepper
200 ml/7 fl oz light cream
6 tbsp grated Parmesan cheese
sautéed white mushrooms,
    to serve

## method

1 Brush 6 x 9-cm/3½-inch soufflé dishes well with melted butter and set aside. Melt the butter in a medium pan, add the flour and cook for 30 seconds, stirring constantly. Whisk in the milk over low heat until the mixture thickens. Cook for a further 30 seconds. Remove from the heat and beat in the ricotta. Add the egg yolks and herbs and season well.

2 Beat the egg whites in a clean bowl until they form stiff peaks and gently fold them through the ricotta mixture. Spoon into the prepared dishes, filling them just to the top. Place in a baking dish and pour in enough boiling water to come halfway up the sides of the dishes. Bake the soufflés in a preheated oven, 180°C/350°F/Gas Mark 4, for 15–20 minutes, or until well risen and browned. Remove from the oven, cool for 10 minutes, then gently ease out of their moulds. Place in a lightly greased ovenproof dish and cover with clingfilm.

3 Increase the oven temperature to 200°C/400°F/Gas Mark 6. Remove the clingfilm and pour the cream evenly over the soufflés, sprinkle with Parmesan and return to the oven for a further 15 minutes. Serve at once with sautéed mushrooms.

# sweet potato, mint & feta patties

## ingredients

### serves 4

600 g/1 lb 5 oz sweet potatoes,
    peeled and grated
1 egg, lightly beaten
50 g/1¾ oz all-purpose flour
70 g/2½ oz butter, melted
100 g/3½ oz feta cheese, crumbled
3 tbsp chopped fresh mint
salt and pepper
1 tbsp vegetable oil
4 tbsp sour cream
2 tbsp chopped fresh parsley,
    to garnish

## method

1 Mix the grated sweet potato with the egg, flour, melted butter, feta and mint until well combined. Season the mixture to taste with salt and pepper.

2 Heat the oil in a large non-stick frying pan over medium heat. Spoon large tablespoons of the mixture into patties, flattening slightly, and cook on both sides in batches until golden brown.

3 Slide the patties onto a baking sheet covered with parchment paper and bake in a preheated oven, 160°C/325°F/Gas Mark 2½, for 15 minutes, or until crisp. Place 2 patties on each plate, top with a tablespoon of sour cream and garnish with a little chopped parsley. Serve at once.

# beans, nuts & tofu

# tuscan bean stew

## ingredients

### serves 4

1 large fennel bulb
2 tbsp olive oil
1 red onion, cut into small wedges
2–4 garlic cloves, sliced
1 fresh green chilli, deseeded
    and chopped
1 small aubergine, about
    225 g/8 oz, cut into chunks
2 tbsp tomato purée
450–600ml/16 fl oz–1 pint
    vegetable stock
450 g/1 lb ripe tomatoes
1 tbsp balsamic vinegar
a few sprigs of fresh oregano
400 g/14 oz canned borlotti beans
400 g/14 oz canned flageolet
    beans
1 yellow pepper, deseeded and cut
    into small strips
1 courgette, sliced into half moons
55 g/2 oz stoned black olives
salt and pepper
25 g/1 oz Parmesan cheese,
    freshly shaved
crusty bread, or polenta wedges,
    to serve

## method

1 Trim the fennel and reserve any feathery fronds, then cut the bulb into small strips. Heat the oil in a large, heavy-based saucepan with a tight-fitting lid, and cook the onion, garlic, chilli, and fennel strips, stirring frequently, for 5–8 minutes, or until softened.

2 Add the aubergine and cook, stirring frequently, for 5 minutes. Blend the tomato purée with a little of the stock in a jug and pour over the fennel mixture, then add the remaining stock, and the tomatoes, vinegar and oregano. Bring to the boil, then reduce the heat and simmer, covered, for 15 minutes, or until the tomatoes have begun to collapse.

3 Drain and rinse the beans, then drain again. Add them to the pan with the yellow pepper, courgette and olives. Simmer for a further 15 minutes, or until all the vegetables are tender. Taste and adjust the seasoning. Scatter with the Parmesan cheese shavings and serve garnished with the reserved fennel fronds, accompanied by crusty bread.

# kidney bean risotto

## ingredients

### serves 4

4 tbsp olive oil
1 onion, chopped
2 garlic cloves, finely chopped
175 g/6 oz brown rice
625 ml/20 fl oz vegetable stock
salt and pepper
1 red pepper, deseeded
    and chopped
2 celery stalks, sliced
225 g/8 oz chestnut mushrooms,
    thinly sliced
425 g/15 oz canned red kidney
    beans, drained
    and rinsed
3 tbsp chopped fresh parsley,
    plus extra to garnish
55 g/2 oz cashews

## method

1 Heat half the oil in a large, heavy-based saucepan. Add the onion and cook, stirring occasionally, for 5 minutes, or until softened. Add half the garlic and cook, stirring frequently, for 2 minutes, then add the rice and stir for 1 minute, or until the grains are thoroughly coated with the oil.

2 Add the stock and a pinch of salt and bring to the boil, stirring constantly. Reduce the heat, cover and simmer for 35–40 minutes, or until all the liquid in the stock has been absorbed.

3 Meanwhile, heat the remaining oil in a heavy-based frying pan. Add the pepper and celery and cook, stirring frequently, for 5 minutes. Add the sliced mushrooms and the remaining garlic and cook, stirring frequently, for 4–5 minutes.

4 Stir the rice into the frying pan. Add the beans, parsley and cashews. Season with salt and pepper and cook, stirring constantly, until hot. Transfer to a warmed serving dish, sprinkle with extra parsley, and serve at once.

# lentil bolognese

## ingredients

serves 4

1 tsp vegetable oil
1 tsp crushed garlic
25 g/1 oz onion, finely chopped
25 g/1 oz leek, finely chopped
25 g/1 oz celery, finely chopped
25 g/1 oz green pepper, deseeded
    and finely chopped
25 g/1 oz carrot, finely chopped
25 g/1 oz courgette, finely
    chopped
85 g/3 oz flat mushrooms, diced
4 tbsp red wine
pinch of dried thyme
400 g/14 oz canned tomatoes,
    chopped, strained through
    a colander, and the juice and
    pulp reserved separately
4 tbsp dried Puy or green lentils,
    cooked
pepper, to taste
2 tsp lemon juice
1 tsp sugar
3 tbsp chopped fresh basil, plus
    extra sprigs to garnish
freshly cooked spaghetti,
    to serve

## method

1 Heat a saucepan over low heat, add the oil and garlic and cook, stirring, until golden brown. Add all the vegetables, except the mushrooms, increase the heat to medium and cook, stirring occasionally, for 10–12 minutes, or until softened and there is no liquid from the vegetables left in the pan.

2 Add the mushrooms, increase the heat to high, add the wine and cook for 2 minutes. Add the thyme and the juice from the tomatoes and cook until reduced by half.

3 Add the lentils and pepper, stir in the tomatoes and cook for a further 3–4 minutes. Remove the pan from the heat and stir in the lemon juice, sugar and basil.

4 Serve the sauce with freshly cooked spaghetti, garnished with basil sprigs.

## variation

Add some kidney beans and chilli flakes and serve with rice to turn this into a lentil and bean chilli.

# spiced lentils with spinach

## ingredients

### serves 4–6

2 tbsp olive oil
1 large onion, finely chopped
1 large garlic clove, crushed
½ tbsp ground cumin
½ tsp ground ginger
250 g/9 oz Puy lentils
about 600 ml/1 pint vegetable
  stock
100 g/3½ oz baby spinach leaves
2 tbsp fresh mint leaves
1 tbsp fresh coriander leaves
1 tbsp fresh flat-leaf parsley
lemon juice
salt and pepper
strips of lemon rind, to garnish

## method

1 Heat the oil in a large frying pan over a medium heat. Add the onion and cook, stirring occasionally, for about 6 minutes. Stir in the garlic, cumin and ginger and cook stirring occasionally, until the onion starts to brown.

2 Stir in the lentils. Pour in enough stock to cover the lentils by 2.5 cm/1 inch and bring to the boil. Lower the heat and simmer for 20–30 minutes until the lentils are tender.

3 Meanwhile, rinse the spinach leaves in several changes of cold water and shake dry. Finely chop the mint, coriander leaves and parsley.

4 If there isn't any stock left in the pan, add a little extra. Add the spinach and stir through until it just wilts. Stir in the mint, coriander and parsley. Adjust the seasoning, adding lemon juice and salt and pepper. Transfer to a serving bowl and serve, garnished with lemon rind.

# warm red lentil salad with goat's cheese

## ingredients

*serves 4*

2 tbsp olive oil
2 tsp cumin seeds
2 garlic cloves, crushed
2 tsp grated fresh ginger
300 g/10½ oz split red lentils
750 ml/24 fl oz vegetable stock
2 tbsp chopped fresh mint
2 tbsp chopped fresh coriander
2 red onions, thinly sliced
200 g/7 oz baby spinach leaves
1 tsp hazelnut oil
150 g/5½ oz soft goat's cheese
4 tbsp Greek-style yogurt
pepper
1 lemon, cut into quarters,
    to garnish
toasted rye bread, to serve

## method

1 Heat half the olive oil in a large saucepan over medium heat, add the cumin seeds, garlic and ginger and cook for 2 minutes, stirring constantly.

2 Stir in the lentils, then add the stock, a ladleful at a time, until it is all absorbed, stirring constantly – this will take about 20 minutes. Remove from the heat and stir in the herbs.

3 Meanwhile, heat the remaining olive oil in a frying pan over medium heat, add the onions and cook, stirring frequently, for 10 minutes, or until soft and lightly browned.

4 Toss the spinach in the hazelnut oil in a bowl, then divide between 4 serving plates.

5 Mash the goat's cheese with the yogurt in a small bowl and season with pepper.

6 Divide the lentils between the serving plates and top with the onions and goat's cheese mixture. Garnish with lemon quarters and serve with toasted rye bread.

# mixed vegetable curry with chickpea pancakes

## ingredients

### serves 4

200 g/7 oz carrots
300 g/10½ oz potatoes
2 tbsp vegetable oil
1½ tsp cumin seeds
seeds from 5 green cardamom
    pods
1½ tsp mustard seeds
2 onions, grated
1 tsp ground turmeric
1 tsp ground coriander
1½ tsp chilli powder
1 bay leaf
1 tbsp grated fresh ginger
2 large garlic cloves, crushed
250 ml/9 fl oz strained tomatoes
200 ml/7 fl oz vegetable stock
115 g/4 oz frozen peas
115 g/4 oz frozen spinach leaves

### chickpea pancakes

225 g/8 oz chickpea flour
1 tsp salt
½ tsp baking soda
400 ml/4 fl oz water
vegetable oil, for cooking

## method

1 To make the pancakes, sift the flour, salt and baking soda into a large bowl. Make a well in the centre and add the water. Using a balloon whisk, gradually mix the flour into the water to form a smooth batter. Set aside for 15 minutes.

2 Heat enough oil to cover the bottom of a frying pan over medium heat. Add a small quantity of batter to the pan, and cook for 3 minutes each side until golden. Repeat with the remaining batter to make 8 pancakes.

3 Meanwhile, cut the carrots into chunks and the potatoes into quarters. Place in a steamer and steam until just tender.

4 Heat the oil in a large saucepan over medium heat and fry the cumin, cardamom and mustard seeds until they start to sizzle. Add the onions, partially cover, and cook over medium–low heat, until soft and golden.

5 Add the other spices, bay leaf, ginger and garlic and cook, stirring, for 1 minute. Add the strained tomatoes, stock, carrots and potatoes, partially cover, and cook for 10–15 minutes, or until the vegetables are tender. Add the peas and spinach, then cook for 2–3 minutes. Serve with the warm pancakes.

# baby corn with dal

## ingredients

### serves 4

225 g/8 oz red split lentils
2 tbsp vegetable oil
1 tsp cumin seeds
1 tsp ground coriander
½ tsp asafetida
1 fresh red chilli, deseeded
    and finely chopped
115 g/4 oz green beans, chopped,
    blanched and drained
1 green pepper, deseeded and
    chopped
115 g/4 oz baby corn, sliced
    diagonally
150 ml/5 fl oz vegetable stock
2 tomatoes, deseeded and
    chopped
1 tbsp chopped fresh coriander
1 tbsp poppy seeds

## method

1 Rinse the lentils 2–3 times in cold water. Put into a large saucepan and cover with cold water. Bring to the boil, then reduce the heat and simmer for 15–20 minutes, or until tender. Drain, return to the pan and keep warm.

2 Meanwhile, heat the oil in a separate saucepan over low heat, add the spices and chilli and cook for 2 minutes, stirring constantly. Add the beans, green pepper and baby corn and cook for 2 minutes, stirring constantly.

3 Stir in the stock and bring to the boil, then reduce the heat and simmer for 5 minutes, or until the vegetables are just tender.

4 Stir the vegetables and their liquid into the cooked lentils with the tomatoes and heat through for 5–8 minutes, or until piping hot.

5 Serve at once, sprinkled with the coriander and poppy seeds.

# bean burgers

## ingredients

*serves 4*

1 tbsp sunflower oil, plus extra
    for brushing
1 onion, finely chopped
1 garlic clove, finely chopped
1 tsp ground coriander
1 tsp ground cumin
115 g/4 oz white mushrooms,
    finely chopped
425 g/15 oz canned borlotti
    or red kidney beans,
    drained and rinsed
2 tbsp chopped fresh flat-leaf
    parsley
salt and pepper
plain flour, for dusting
hamburger buns
salad, to serve

## method

1 Heat the oil in a heavy-based frying pan over medium
    heat. Add the onion and cook, stirring frequently, for
    5 minutes, or until softened. Add the garlic, coriander
    and cumin and cook, stirring, for a further minute.
    Add the mushrooms and cook, stirring frequently, for
    4–5 minutes until all the liquid has evaporated. Transfer
    to a bowl.

2 Put the beans in a small bowl and mash with a fork.
    Stir into the mushroom mixture with the parsley and
    season with salt and pepper.

3 Preheat the grill to medium–high. Divide the mixture
    equally into 4 portions, dust lightly with flour and
    shape into flat, round patties. Brush with oil and cook
    under the grill for 4–5 minutes on each side. Serve in
    hamburger buns with salad.

# chilli bean cakes with avocado salsa

## ingredients

### serves 4

55 g/2 oz pine nuts
425 g/15 oz canned mixed beans, drained and rinsed
½ red onion, finely chopped
1 tbsp tomato purée
½ fresh red chilli, deseeded and finely chopped
55 g/2 oz brown breadcrumbs
1 egg, beaten
1 tbsp finely chopped coriander
2 tbsp corn oil
1 lime, cut into quarters, to garnish
4 toasted wholewheat bread rolls, to serve (optional)

### salsa

1 avocado, stoned, peeled and chopped
100 g/3½ oz tomatoes, deseeded and chopped
2 garlic cloves, crushed
2 tbsp finely chopped coriander
1 tbsp olive oil
pepper
juice of ½ lime

## method

1 Heat a non-stick frying pan over medium heat, add the pine nuts and cook, turning, until just browned. Immediately tip into a bowl and set aside.

2 Put the beans into a large bowl and coarsely mash. Add the onion, tomato purée, chilli, pine nuts and half the breadcrumbs and mix well. Add half the egg and the coriander and mash together, adding a little more egg, if needed, to bind the mixture. Form the mixture into 4 flat cakes. Coat with the remaining breadcrumbs, cover and chill in the refrigerator for 30 minutes.

3 To make the salsa, mix all the ingredients together in a serving bowl, cover and chill in the refrigerator until required.

4 Heat the oil in a frying pan over medium heat, add the bean cakes and cook for 4–5 minutes on each side, or until crisp and heated through. Remove from the pan and drain on kitchen paper.

5 Serve each bean cake in a toasted whole-wheat roll, if desired, with the salsa, garnished with a lime quarter.

# toasted pine nut & vegetable couscous

## ingredients

### serves 4

115 g/4 oz dried green lentils
55 g/2 oz pine nuts
1 tbsp olive oil
1 onion, diced
2 garlic cloves, crushed
280 g/10 oz courgettes, sliced
250 g/9 oz tomatoes, chopped
400 g/14 oz canned artichoke
    hearts, drained and cut in half
    lengthways
250 g/9 oz couscous
500 ml/16 fl oz vegetable stock
3 tbsp torn fresh basil leaves, plus
    extra leaves to garnish
pepper

## method

1 Put the lentils into a saucepan with plenty of cold water, bring to the boil and boil rapidly for 10 minutes. Reduce the heat, cover and simmer until tender.

2 Meanwhile, preheat the grill to medium. Spread the pine nuts out in a single layer on a baking sheet and toast under the preheated grill, turning to brown evenly – watch constantly because they brown very quickly. Tip the pine nuts into a small dish and set aside.

3 Heat the oil in a frying pan over medium heat, add the onion, garlic and courgettes and cook, stirring frequently, for 8–10 minutes, or until tender and the courgettes have browned slightly. Add the tomatoes and artichoke halves and heat through thoroughly.

4 Meanwhile, put the couscous into a heatproof bowl. Bring the stock to the boil in a saucepan and pour over the couscous, cover and stand for 10 minutes until the couscous absorbs the stock and becomes tender.

5 Drain the lentils and stir into the couscous. Stir in the torn basil leaves and season well with pepper. Transfer to a warmed serving dish and spoon over the cooked vegetables. Sprinkle the pine nuts over the top, garnish with basil leaves and serve at once.

# falafel burgers

## ingredients

### serves 4

2 x 400-g/14-oz cans chickpeas,
    drained and rinsed
1 small onion, chopped
zest and juice of 1 lime
2 tsp ground coriander
2 tsp ground cumin
6 tbsp plain flour
4 tbsp olive oil
4 sprigs fresh basil,
    to garnish
tomato salsa, to serve

## method

1 Put the chickpeas, onion, lime zest and juice and
    the spices into a food processor and process to
    a coarse paste.

2 Tip the mixture out onto a clean work surface
    or chopping board and shape into 4 patties.

3 Spread the flour out on a large flat plate and use
    to coat the patties.

4 Heat the oil in a large frying pan, add the burgers and
    cook for 2 minutes on each side until crisp. Garnish
    with basil and serve with tomato salsa.

# wilted spinach, yogurt & walnut salad

## ingredients

*serves 2*

450 g/1 lb fresh spinach leaves
1 onion, chopped
1 tbsp olive oil
225 ml/8 fl oz natural yogurt
1 garlic clove, finely chopped
2 tbsp chopped toasted walnuts
2–3 tsp chopped fresh mint
salt and pepper
pitta bread, to serve

## method

1 Put the spinach and onion into a saucepan, cover and cook gently for a few minutes until the spinach has wilted.

2 Add the oil and cook for a further 5 minutes. Season to taste with salt and pepper.

3 Combine the yogurt and garlic in a bowl.

4 Put the spinach and onion into a serving bowl and pour over the yogurt mixture. Scatter over the walnuts and chopped mint and serve with pitta bread.

# celeriac, chestnut, spinach & feta filo pies

## ingredients

### serves 4

4 tbsp olive oil

2 garlic cloves, crushed

½ large or 1 whole small head celeriac, cut into short thin sticks

250 g/9 oz baby spinach leaves

85 g/3 oz cooked, peeled chestnuts, coarsely chopped

200 g/7 oz Feta cheese (drained weight), crumbled

1 egg

2 tbsp pesto sauce

1 tbsp finely chopped fresh parsley

pepper

4 sheets filo pastry, about 32 x 18 cm/13 x 7 inches each

## method

1 Heat 1 tablespoon of the oil in a large frying pan over medium heat, add the garlic and cook for 1 minute, stirring constantly. Add the celeriac and cook for 5 minutes, or until soft and browned. Remove from the pan and keep warm.

2 Add 1 tablespoon of the remaining oil to the frying pan, then add the spinach, cover and cook for 2–3 minutes, or until the spinach has wilted. Uncover and cook until any liquid has evaporated.

3 Mix the garlic and celeriac, spinach, chestnuts, cheese, egg, pesto, parsley and pepper in a large bowl. Divide the mixture between 4 individual gratin dishes or put it all into 1 medium gratin dish.

4 Brush each sheet of filo with the remaining oil and arrange, slightly scrunched, on top of the celeriac mixture. Bake in a preheated oven, 190°C/375°F/Gas Mark 5, for 15–20 minutes, or until browned. Serve at once.

# nutty stilton roast

## ingredients

### serves 6–8

2 tbsp virgin olive oil,
    plus extra for oiling
2 onions, one finely chopped
    and one cut into
    thin wedges
3–5 garlic cloves, crushed
2 celery stalks, finely sliced
175 g/6 oz cooked and peeled
    chestnuts
175 g/6 oz mixed chopped nuts
55 g/2 oz ground almonds
55 g/2 oz fresh wholewheat
    breadcrumbs
225 g/8 oz Stilton cheese,
    crumbled
1 tbsp chopped fresh basil, plus
    extra sprigs to garnish
1 egg, beaten
salt and pepper
1 red pepper, peeled, deseeded
    and cut into thin wedges
1 courgette, about 115 g/4 oz,
    cut into wedges
cherry tomatoes, to garnish
tomato ketchup, to serve

## method

1 Heat 1 tablespoon of the oil in a frying pan over
    medium heat, add the chopped onion, 1–2 of the garlic
    cloves, and the celery and cook for 5 minutes, stirring
    occasionally.

2 Remove from the pan, drain through a sieve and
    transfer to a food processor with the nuts, breadcrumbs,
    half the cheese and the basil. Using the pulse button,
    blend the ingredients together, then slowly blend in
    the egg to form a stiff mixture. Season.

3 Heat the remaining oil in a frying pan over medium
    heat, add the onion wedges, remaining garlic, red
    pepper and courgette and cook for 5 minutes, stirring
    frequently. Remove from the pan, add salt and pepper
    and drain through a sieve.

4 Place half the nut mixture in a lightly oiled 900-g/2-lb
    loaf pan and smooth the surface. Cover with the onion
    and pepper mixture and crumble over the remaining
    cheese. Top with the remaining nut mixture and press
    down firmly. Cover with foil. Bake in a preheated oven,
    180°C/350°F/Gas Mark 4, for 45 minutes. Remove the
    foil and bake for a further 25–35 minutes, until firm.

5 Remove from the oven, cool in the pan for 5 minutes,
    then turn out and serve in slices garnished with basil
    sprigs, cherry tomatoes and a little tomato ketchup.

# vegetable & hazelnut loaf

## ingredients

### serves 4

2 tbsp sunflower oil, plus extra
    for oiling
1 onion, chopped
1 garlic clove, finely chopped
2 celery stalks, chopped
1 tbsp plain flour
200 ml/7 fl oz strained canned
    tomatoes
115 g/4 oz fresh wholewheat
    breadcrumbs
2 carrots, grated
115 g/4 oz toasted hazelnuts,
    ground
1 tbsp dark soy sauce
2 tbsp chopped fresh coriander
1 egg, lightly beaten
salt and pepper
mixed red and green lettuce leaves,
    to serve

## method

1 Oil and line a 450-g/1-lb loaf pan. Heat the oil in a heavy-based frying pan over medium heat. Add the onion and cook, stirring frequently, for 5 minutes, or until softened. Add the garlic and celery and cook, stirring frequently, for 5 minutes. Add the flour and cook stirring constantly, for 1 minute. Gradually stir in the strained canned tomatoes and cook, stirring constantly, until thickened. Remove the pan from the heat.

2 Put the breadcrumbs, carrots, ground hazelnuts, soy sauce and coriander in a bowl. Add the tomato mixture and stir well. Cool slightly, then beat in the egg and season with salt and pepper.

3 Spoon the mixture into the prepared pan and smooth the surface. Cover with foil and bake in a preheated oven, 180°C/350°F/Gas Mark 4, for 1 hour. If serving hot, turn the loaf out on to a warmed serving dish and serve immediately with mixed red and green salad leaves. Alternatively, cool the loaf in the pan before turning out.

# tofu stir-fry

## ingredients

*serves 4*

2 tbsp sunflower or olive oil
350 g/12 oz firm tofu, cubed
225 g/8 oz pak choi, roughly
chopped
1 garlic clove, chopped
4 tbsp sweet chilli sauce
2 tbsp light soy sauce

## method

*1* Heat 1 tablespoon of oil in a wok, add the tofu in
batches and stir-fry for 2–3 minutes until golden.
Remove and set aside.

*2* Add the pak choi to the wok and stir-fry for a few
seconds until tender and wilted. Remove and set aside

*3* Add the remaining oil to the wok, then add the garlic
and stir-fry for 30 seconds.

*4* Stir in the chilli sauce and soy sauce and bring to
the boil.

*5* Return the tofu and pak choi to the wok and toss
gently until coated in the sauce. Serve immediately.

# thai tofu cakes with chilli dip

## ingredients

### serves 8

300 g/10½ oz firm tofu, drained weight, coarsely grated

1 lemon grass stalk, outer layer discarded, finely chopped

2 garlic cloves, chopped

2.5-cm/1-inch piece fresh ginger, grated

2 kaffir lime leaves, finely chopped

2 shallots, finely chopped

2 fresh red chillies, deseeded and finely chopped

4 tbsp chopped fresh coriander

90 g/3¼ oz gluten-free plain flour, plus extra for flouring

½ tsp salt

corn oil, for cooking

### chilli dip

3 tbsp white distilled vinegar or rice wine vinegar

2 spring onions, finely sliced

1 tbsp caster sugar

2 fresh chillies, finely chopped

2 tbsp chopped fresh coriander

pinch of salt

## method

1 To make the chilli dip, mix all the ingredients together in a small serving bowl and set aside.

2 Mix the tofu with the lemon grass, garlic, ginger, lime leaves, if using, shallots, chillies and coriander in a mixing bowl. Stir in the flour and salt to make a coarse sticky paste. Cover and chill in the refrigerator for 1 hour to let the mixture firm up slightly.

3 Form the mixture into 8 large walnut-size balls and, using floured hands, flatten into circles. Heat enough oil to cover the bottom of a large, heavy-based frying pan over medium heat. Cook the cakes in 2 batches, turning halfway through, for 4–6 minutes, or until golden brown. Drain on kitchen paper and serve warm with the chilli dip.

# pasta, noodles & rice

# pasta with olive sauce

## ingredients

### serves 2–4

350 g/12 oz fresh pasta shapes
6 tbsp olive oil
½ tsp freshly grated nutmeg
½ tsp black pepper
1 garlic clove, crushed
2 tbsp tapenade
85 g/3 oz black or green olives,
    stoned and sliced
1 tbsp chopped fresh parsley,
    to garnish (optional)
salt

## method

1 Cook the pasta in a large saucepan of boiling salted
water for about 4 minutes, or according to the packet
instructions until tender but still firm to the bite.

2 Meanwhile, put ½ teaspoon of salt with the oil,
nutmeg, pepper, garlic, tapenade and olives in another
saucepan and heat slowly but don't allow to boil.
Cover and leave to stand for 3–4 minutes.

3 Drain the pasta and return to the saucepan. Add the
flavoured oil and heat gently for 1–2 minutes. Serve
immediately garnished, with chopped parsley, if using.

# macaroni & cheese

## ingredients

### serves 4

225 g/8 oz macaroni
1 egg, beaten
125 g/4½ oz mature Cheddar
    cheese, grated
1 tbsp wholegrain mustard
2 tbsp chopped fresh chives
béchamel sauce (see below)
salt and pepper
4 tomatoes, sliced
125 g/4½ oz Red Leicester
    cheese, grated
60 g/2¼ oz blue cheese, grated
2 tbsp sunflower seeds
snipped fresh chives,
    to garnish

### béchamel sauce

625 ml/20 fl oz milk
1 bay leaf
6 black peppercorns
slice of onion
mace blade
4 tbsp butter
2 tbsp plain flour
salt and pepper

## method

1 To make the béchamel sauce, pour the milk into a
saucepan. Add the bay leaf, peppercorns, onion and
mace. Heat to just below boiling point, then remove
from the heat, cover, infuse for 10 minutes, then strain.
Melt the butter in a separate saucepan. Sprinkle in the
flour and cook over low heat, stirring constantly, for
1 minute. Stir in the milk, then bring to the boil and
cook, stirring, until thickened and smooth. Season.

2 Bring a large pan of lightly salted water to the boil
and cook the macaroni for 8–10 minutes, or until just
tender. Drain well and place in an ovenproof dish.

3 Stir the beaten egg, Cheddar cheese, mustard and
chives into the béchamel sauce and season with salt
and pepper. Spoon the mixture over the macaroni,
making sure it is well covered. Top with a layer of the
sliced tomatoes.

4 Sprinkle the Red Leicester cheese, blue cheese and
sunflower seeds over the top. Place on a baking sheet
and bake in a preheated oven, 190°C/375°F/Gas Mark 5,
for 25–30 minutes, or until bubbling and golden.
Garnish with snipped fresh chives and serve at once.

# vegetarian lasagna

## ingredients

*serves 4*

olive oil, for brushing
2 aubergines, sliced
2 tbsp butter
1 garlic clove, finely chopped
4 courgettes, sliced
1 tbsp finely chopped fresh
    flat-leaf parsley and marjoram
225 g/8 oz mozzarella cheese,
    grated
625 ml/20 fl oz strained canned
    tomatoes
175 g/6 oz dried no-precook
    lasagna
salt and pepper
béchamel sauce (see below)
55 g/2 oz freshly grated Parmesan
    cheese

### béchamel sauce

300 ml/10 fl oz milk
1 bay leaf
6 black peppercorns
slice of onion
mace blade
2 tbsp butter
3 tbsp plain flour
salt and pepper

## method

1 To make the béchamel sauce, pour the milk into a saucepan. Add the bay leaf, peppercorns, onion and mace. Heat to just below boiling point, then remove from the heat, cover, infuse for 10 minutes, then strain. Melt the butter in a separate saucepan. Sprinkle in the flour and cook over low heat, stirring constantly, for 1 minute. Stir in the milk, then bring to the boil and cook, stirring, until thickened and smooth. Season.

2 Brush a grill pan with olive oil and heat until smoking. Add half the aubergine slices and cook over medium heat for 8 minutes, or until golden brown all over. Remove from the grill pan and drain on kitchen paper. Repeat with the remaining aubergine slices.

3 Melt the butter in a frying pan and add the garlic, courgettes, parsley and marjoram. Cook over medium heat, stirring frequently, for 5 minutes, or until the courgettes are golden all over. Drain on kitchen paper.

4 Layer the aubergine, courgettes, mozzarella, tomatoes and lasagna in an ovenproof dish brushed with olive oil, seasoning as you go and finishing with a layer of lasagna. Pour over the béchamel sauce, making sure that all the pasta is covered. Sprinkle with Parmesan cheese and bake in a preheated oven, 200°C/400°F/ Gas Mark 6, for 30–40 minutes, or until golden brown.

# pasta with pesto

## ingredients

### serves 4

450 g/1 lb dried tagliatelle
fresh basil sprigs, to garnish

### pesto

2 garlic cloves
25 g/1 oz pine nuts
salt
115 g/4 oz fresh basil leaves
55 g/2 oz freshly grated Parmesan
    cheese
125 ml/4 fl oz olive oil

## method

1 To make the pesto, put the garlic, pine nuts, a large pinch of salt and the basil into a mortar and pound to a paste with a pestle. Transfer to a bowl and gradually work in the Parmesan cheese with a wooden spoon, followed by the olive oil, to make a thick, creamy sauce. Taste and adjust the seasoning if necessary.

2 Alternatively, put the garlic, pine nuts and a large pinch of salt into a food processor or blender and process briefly. Add the basil leaves and process to a paste. With the motor still running, gradually add the olive oil. Scrape into a bowl and beat in the Parmesan cheese.

3 Bring a large pan of lightly salted water to the boil. Add the pasta, return to the boil and cook for 8–10 minutes, or until tender but still firm to the bite. Drain the pasta well, return to the pan, and toss with half the pesto, then divide between warmed serving plates and top with the remaining pesto. Garnish with basil sprigs and serve immediately.

# creamy spinach & mushroom pasta

## ingredients

### serves 4

300 g/10½ oz dried
   gluten-free penne or
   pasta of your choice
2 tbsp olive oil
250 g/9 oz mushrooms, sliced
1 tsp dried oregano
275 ml/9 fl oz vegetable stock
1 tbsp lemon juice
6 tbsp cream cheese
200 g/7 oz frozen spinach leaves
salt and pepper

## method

1 Cook the pasta in a large pan of lightly salted boiling water, according to the packet instructions. Drain, reserving 175 ml/6 fl oz of the cooking liquid.

2 Meanwhile, heat the oil in a large, heavy-based frying pan over medium heat, add the mushrooms and cook, stirring frequently, for 8 minutes, or until almost crisp. Stir in the oregano, stock and lemon juice and cook for 10–12 minutes, or until the sauce is reduced by half.

3 Stir in the cream cheese and spinach and cook over medium–low heat for 3–5 minutes. Add the reserved cooking liquid, then the cooked pasta. Stir well, season to taste with salt and pepper and heat through gently before serving.

# crisp noodle & vegetable stir-fry

## ingredients

### serves 4

peanut or sunflower oil,
  for deep-frying
115 g/4 oz rice vermicelli,
  broken into 7.5-cm/
  3-inch lengths
115 g/4 oz green beans,
  cut into short lengths
2 carrots, cut into thin sticks
2 courgettes, cut into thin sticks
115 g/4 oz shiitake mushrooms,
  sliced
2.5-cm/1-inch piece fresh
  ginger, shredded
½ small head Napa cabbage,
  shredded
4 spring onions, shredded
85 g/3 oz beansprouts
2 tbsp dark soy sauce
2 tbsp Chinese rice wine
large pinch of sugar
2 tbsp coarsely chopped
  fresh coriander

## method

1 Half-fill a wok or deep, heavy-based frying pan with oil. Heat to 180–190°C/350–375°F, or until a cube of bread browns in 30 seconds.

2 Add the noodles, in batches, and cook for 1½–2 minutes, or until crisp and puffed up. Remove and drain on kitchen paper. Pour off all but 2 tablespoons of oil from the wok.

3 Heat the remaining oil over a high heat. Add the green beans and stir-fry for 2 minutes. Add the carrot and courgette sticks, the sliced mushrooms and ginger and stir-fry for a further 2 minutes.

4 Add the shredded Napa cabbage, spring onions and beansprouts and stir-fry for a further minute. Add the soy sauce, rice wine and sugar and cook, stirring constantly, for 1 minute.

5 Add the chopped coriander and toss well. Serve immediately, with the noodles.

# chinese vegetables & beansprouts with noodles

## ingredients

### serves 4

1.25 litres/40 fl oz vegetable stock
1 garlic clove, crushed
1-cm/½-inch piece fresh
    ginger, finely chopped
225 g/8 oz dried medium
    egg noodles
1 red pepper, deseeded
    and sliced
85 g/3 oz frozen peas
115 g/4 oz broccoli florets
85 g/3 oz shiitake mushrooms,
    sliced
2 tbsp sesame seeds
225 g/8 oz canned water
    chestnuts, drained
    and halved
225 g/8 oz canned bamboo
    shoots, drained
280 g/10 oz Napa cabbage, sliced
140 g/5 oz beansprouts
3 spring onions, sliced
1 tbsp dark soy sauce
pepper

## method

1 Bring the stock, garlic and ginger to the boil in a large saucepan. Stir in the noodles, red pepper, peas, brocco and mushrooms and return to the boil. Reduce the heat, cover, and simmer for 5–6 minutes, or until the noodles are tender.

2 Meanwhile, preheat the grill to medium. Spread the sesame seeds out in a single layer on a baking sheet ar toast under the preheated grill, turning to brown even – watch constantly because they brown very quickly. Tip the sesame seeds into a small dish and set aside.

3 Once the noodles are tender, add the water chestnut bamboo shoots, Napa cabbage, beansprouts and spring onions to the pan. Return the stock to the boil stir to mix the ingredients and simmer for a further 2–3 minutes to heat through thoroughly.

4 Carefully drain off 300 ml/10 fl oz of the stock into a small heatproof jug and set aside. Drain and discard any remaining stock and turn the noodles and vegetables into a warmed serving dish. Quickly mix the soy sauce with the reserved stock and pour over the noodles and vegetables. Season with peppe and serve at once.

# sweet & sour vegetables on noodle pancakes

## ingredients

### serves 4

115 g/4 oz dried thin
  cellophane noodles
6 eggs
4 spring onions, sliced diagonally
salt and pepper
2½ tbsp peanut or corn oil
900 g/2 lb selection of vegetables,
  such as carrots, baby corn,
  cauliflower, broccoli,
  mangetout and onions, peeled
  as necessary and chopped
  into same-size pieces
100 g/3½ oz canned bamboo
  shoots, drained
200 g/7 oz bottled sweet-&-sour
  sauce

## method

1 Soak the noodles in enough lukewarm water to cover and stand for 20 minutes, until soft. Alternatively, cook according to the packet instructions. Drain them well and use scissors to cut into 7.5-cm/3-inch pieces, then set aside.

2 Beat the eggs, then stir in the noodles, spring onions, salt and pepper. Heat a 20-cm/8-inch frying pan over high heat. Add 1 tablespoon oil and swirl it round. Pour in a quarter of the egg mixture and tilt the pan so it covers the bottom. Lower the heat to medium and cook for 1 minute, or until the thin pancake is set. Flip it over, adding a little extra oil, if necessary, and cook the other side until golden. Keep warm in a low oven while you make 3 more pancakes.

3 After you've made 4 pancakes, heat a wok or large, heavy-based frying pan over high heat. Add 1½ tablespoons oil and heat until it shimmers. Add the thickest vegetables, such as carrots, first and stir-fry for 30 seconds. Gradually add the remaining vegetables and bamboo shoots. Stir in the sauce and stir-fry until all the vegetables are tender and the sauce is hot. Spoon the vegetables and sauce over the pancakes and serve.

# wild mushroom risotto

## ingredients

### serves 6

55 g/2 oz dried porcini or morel
    mushrooms
about 500 g/1 lb 2 oz mixed fresh
    wild mushrooms, such as
    porcini, horse mushrooms and
    chanterelles, halved if large
4 tbsp olive oil
3–4 garlic cloves,
    finely chopped
55 g/2 oz butter
1 onion, finely chopped
350 g/12 oz Arborio rice
50 ml/2 fl oz dry
    white vermouth
1.25 litres/40 fl oz simmering
    vegetable stock
salt and pepper
115 g/4 oz freshly grated
    Parmesan cheese
4 tbsp chopped fresh
    flat-leaf parsley

## method

1 Place the dried mushrooms in a heatproof bowl
and add boiling water to cover. Set aside to soak for
30 minutes, then carefully lift out and pat dry. Strain the
soaking liquid through a sieve lined with kitchen paper
and set aside.

2 Heat 3 tablespoons of the oil in a large frying pan.
Add the fresh mushrooms and stir-fry for 1–2 minutes.
Add the garlic and the soaked mushrooms and cook,
stirring frequently, for 2 minutes. Transfer to a plate.

3 Heat the remaining oil and half the butter in
a pan. Add the onion and cook over medium heat,
stirring, until softened. Reduce the heat, add the rice and
cook, stirring, until the grains are translucent. Add the
vermouth and cook, stirring, for 1 minute until reduced.

4 Gradually add the hot stock, a ladleful at a time. Stir
constantly and add more liquid as the rice absorbs
each addition. Increase the heat to medium so that
the liquid bubbles. Cook for 20 minutes, or until all
the liquid is absorbed and the rice is creamy.

5 Add half the reserved mushroom soaking liquid
and stir in the mushrooms. Season and add more
mushroom liquid, if necessary. Remove from the heat,
stir in the remaining butter, the grated Parmesan and
the chopped parsley and serve at once.

# risotto primavera

## ingredients

### serves 6–8

225 g/8 oz fresh thin asparagus spears
4 tbsp olive oil
175 g/6 oz young green beans, cut into 2.5-cm/1-inch lengths
175 g/6 oz young courgettes, quartered and cut into 2.5-cm/1-inch lengths
225 g/8 oz shelled fresh peas
1 onion, finely chopped
1–2 garlic cloves, finely chopped
350 g/12 oz Arborio rice
1.6 litres/52 fl oz simmering vegetable stock
4 spring onions, cut into 2.5-cm/1-inch lengths
salt and pepper
55 g/2 oz butter
115 g/4 oz freshly grated Parmesan cheese
2 tbsp snipped fresh chives
2 tbsp shredded fresh basil
spring onions, to garnish (optional)

## method

1 Trim the woody ends of the asparagus and cut off the tips. Cut the stems into 2.5-cm/1-inch pieces and set aside with the tips. Heat 2 tablespoons of the oil in a large frying pan over high heat until very hot. Add the asparagus, beans, courgettes and peas and stir-fry for 3–4 minutes until they are bright green and just starting to soften. Set aside.

2 Heat the remaining oil in a large, heavy-based pan over medium heat. Add the onion and cook, stirring occasionally, for 3 minutes, or until it starts to soften. Stir in the garlic and cook, while stirring, for 30 seconds Reduce the heat, add the rice and mix to coat in oil. Cook, stirring constantly, for 2–3 minutes, or until the grains are translucent.

3 Add the hot stock, a ladleful at a time. Stir constantly and add more liquid as the rice absorbs each addition. Increase the heat to medium so that the liquid bubbles. Cook for 20 minutes, or until all but 2 tablespoons of the liquid is absorbed and the rice is creamy.

4 Stir in the stir-fried vegetables, onion mixture and spring onions with the remaining stock. Cook for 2 minutes, stirring frequently. Stir in the butter, Parmesan, chives and basil. Serve the risotto at once, garnished with spring onions, if liked.

# spiced risotto cakes

## ingredients

### serves 3

85 g/3 oz onion, finely chopped
85 g/3 oz leek, finely chopped
25 g/1 oz Arborio rice
550 ml/18 fl oz vegetable stock
85 g/3 oz grated courgette
1 tbsp fresh basil, chopped
25 g/1 oz fresh wholewheat
   breadcrumbs
vegetable oil spray
radicchio leaves, to serve

### filling

50 g/1¾ oz cream cheese
50 g/1¾ oz mango, diced
1 tsp finely grated lime rind
1 tsp lime juice
pinch of cayenne pepper

## method

1 Heat a large, non-stick pan over high heat, add the onion and leek, and cook, stirring constantly, for 2–3 minutes, or until softened but not coloured.

2 Add the rice and stock, bring to the boil, then continue to boil, stirring constantly, for 2 minutes. Reduce the heat and cook for a further 15 minutes, stirring every 2–3 minutes. When the rice is nearly cooked and has absorbed all the stock, stir in the courgette and basil and cook, continuing to stir, over high heat for a further 5–10 minutes or until the mixture is sticky and dry. Turn out onto a plate and let cool.

3 Meanwhile, to make the filling, mix the cream cheese, mango, lime rind and juice and cayenne together in a bowl.

4 Divide the cooled rice mixture into 3 and form into cakes. Make an indentation in the centre of each cake and fill with 1 tablespoon of the filling. Mould the sides up and over to seal in the filling, then reshape with a palette knife. Coat each cake with breadcrumbs and arrange on a non-stick baking sheet. Spray each cake lightly with oil and bake in a preheated oven, 200°C/400°F/Gas Mark 6, for 15–20 minutes, or until a light golden brown colour. Serve with radicchio leaves.

# spicy stuffed peppers

## ingredients

### serves 4

4 assorted coloured peppers
3 sprays olive oil
1 onion, finely chopped
2 garlic cloves, chopped
2.5-cm/1-inch piece fresh
    ginger, peeled and grated
1–2 fresh serrano chillies,
    deseeded and chopped
1 tsp ground cumin
1 tsp ground coriander
85 g/3 oz cooked brown
    basmati rice
1 large carrot, about 115 g/4 oz,
    peeled and grated
1 large courgette, about 85 g/3 oz,
    trimmed and grated
25 g/1 oz ready-to-eat dried
    apricots, finely chopped
1 tbsp chopped fresh coriander
150 ml/5 fl oz water
pepper
fresh herbs, to garnish

## method

1 Cut the tops off the peppers and reserve. Discard the seeds from each pepper. Place the peppers in a large bowl and cover with boiling water. Leave to soak for 10 minutes then drain and reserve.

2 Heat a non-stick frying pan and spray with the oil. Add the onion, garlic, ginger and chillies and sauté for 3 minutes, stirring frequently. Sprinkle in the ground spices and continue to cook for a further 2 minutes.

3 Remove the pan from the heat and stir in the rice, carrot, courgette, apricots, chopped coriander, and pepper to taste. Stir well, then use to stuff the peppers.

4 Place the stuffed peppers in an ovenproof dish large enough to allow the peppers to stand upright. Put the reserved tops in position. Pour the water around their bases, cover loosely with the lid or foil and bake in a preheated oven, 190°C/375°F/Gas Mark 5, for 25–30 minutes, or until piping hot. Serve garnished with herbs.

# stir-fried rice with green vegetables

## ingredients

*serves 4*

225 g/8 oz jasmine rice
2 tbsp vegetable or peanut oil
1 tbsp green curry paste
6 spring onions, sliced
2 garlic cloves, crushed
1 courgette, cut into thin sticks
115 g/4 oz green beans
175 g/6 oz asparagus, trimmed
3–4 fresh Thai basil leaves

## method

1 Cook the rice in lightly salted boiling water for 12–15 minutes, drain well, then cool thoroughly and chill overnight.

2 Heat the oil in a wok and stir-fry the curry paste for 1 minute. Add the spring onions and garlic and stir-fry for 1 minute.

3 Add the courgette, beans and asparagus and stir-fry for 3–4 minutes, until just tender. Break up the rice and add it to the wok. Cook, stirring constantly for 2–3 minutes, until the rice is hot. Stir in the basil leaves. Serve hot.

## variation

Use red curry paste and red or orange vegetables such a red peppers and carrots to make a delicious variation to this recipe.

# vegetable biryani

## ingredients

### serves 4

2 tbsp vegetable oil
3 whole cloves
3 cardamom pods, cracked
1 onion, chopped
115 g/4 oz carrots, chopped
2–3 garlic cloves, crushed
1–2 fresh red chillies, deseeded
    and chopped
2.5-cm/1-inch piece fresh
    ginger, grated
115 g/4 oz cauliflower, broken into
    small florets
175 g/6 oz broccoli, broken into
    small florets
115 g/4 oz green beans, chopped
400 g/14 oz canned chopped
    tomatoes
150 ml/5 fl oz vegetable stock
salt and pepper
115 g/4 oz okra, sliced
1 tbsp chopped fresh coriander,
    plus extra sprigs to garnish
115 g/4 oz brown basmati rice
few saffron threads (optional)
grated lime rind, to garnish

## method

1 Heat the oil in a large pan over low heat, add the spices, onion, carrots, garlic, chillies and ginger and cook, stirring frequently, for 5 minutes.

2 Add the cauliflower, broccoli and green beans and cook, stirring frequently, for 5 minutes. Stir in the tomatoes, stock, salt and pepper and bring to the boil. Reduce the heat, cover and simmer for 10 minutes.

3 Add the okra and cook for a further 8–10 minutes, or until the vegetables are tender. Stir in the coriander. Strain off any excess liquid and keep warm.

4 Meanwhile, cook the rice with the saffron in a pan of lightly salted boiling water for 25 minutes, or until tender. Drain and keep warm.

5 Layer the vegetables and cooked rice in a deep dish or ovenproof bowl, packing the layers down firmly. Let stand for about 5 minutes, then invert onto a warmed serving dish and serve, garnished with grated lime rind and coriander sprigs, with the reserved liquid.

# vegetarian paella

## ingredients

### serves 4-6

½ tsp saffron threads

2 tbsp hot water

6 tbsp olive oil

1 Spanish onion, sliced

3 garlic cloves, minced

1 red pepper, deseeded and sliced

1 orange pepper, deseeded
    and sliced

1 large aubergine, cubed

200 g/7 oz medium-grain
    paella rice

625 ml/20 fl oz vegetable stock

450 g/1 lb tomatoes, peeled
    and chopped

salt and pepper

115 g/4 oz mushrooms, sliced

115 g/4 oz green beans, halved

400 g/14 oz canned
    borlotti beans

## method

1　Put the saffron threads and water in a small bowl
    or cup and infuse for a few minutes.

2　Meanwhile, heat the oil in a paella pan or wide, shallow
    frying pan and cook the onion over medium heat,
    stirring, for 2–3 minutes, or until softened. Add the
    garlic, peppers and aubergine and cook, stirring
    frequently, for 5 minutes.

3　Add the rice and cook, stirring constantly,
    for 1 minute, or until glossy and coated. Pour in the
    stock and add the tomatoes, saffron and its soaking
    water, salt and pepper. Bring to the boil, then reduce
    the heat and simmer, shaking the pan frequently and
    stirring occasionally, for 15 minutes.

4　Stir in the mushrooms, green beans and borlotti beans
    with their can juices. Cook for a further 10 minutes,
    then serve immediately.

# artichoke paella

## ingredients

### serves 4–6

½ tsp saffron threads

2 tbsp hot water

3 tbsp olive oil

1 large onion, chopped

1 courgette, coarsely chopped

2 garlic cloves, crushed

¼ tsp cayenne pepper

225 g/8 oz tomatoes, peeled and
    cut into wedges

425 g/15 oz canned chickpeas,
    drained

425 g/15 oz canned artichokes
    hearts, drained and coarsely
    sliced

350 g/12 oz medium-grain
    paella rice

1.3 litres/42 fl oz simmering
    vegetable stock

150 g/5½ oz green beans,
    blanched

salt and pepper

1 lemon, cut into wedges,
    to serve

## method

1 Put the saffron threads and water in a small bowl and
    infuse for a few minutes.

2 Meanwhile, heat the oil in a paella pan and cook the
    onion and courgette over medium heat, stirring, for
    2–3 minutes, or until softened. Add the garlic, cayenne
    pepper and saffron and its soaking liquid and cook,
    stirring constantly, for 1 minute. Add the tomato
    wedges, chickpeas and artichokes and cook, stirring,
    for a further 2 minutes.

3 Add the rice and cook, stirring constantly, for 1 minute
    or until the rice is glossy and coated. Pour in most
    of the hot stock and bring to the boil, then simmer,
    uncovered, for 10 minutes. Do not stir during cooking,
    but shake the pan once or twice. Add the green beans
    and season. Shake the pan and cook for a further
    10–15 minutes, or until the rice grains are plump and
    cooked. If needed, pour in a little more hot stock, then
    shake the pan to spread the liquid through the paella.

4 When all the liquid has been absorbed and you detect
    a faint toasty aroma coming from the rice, remove from
    the heat immediately to prevent burning. Cover the
    pan with a clean tea towel or foil and let stand for
    5 minutes. Serve direct from the pan with the lemon
    wedges to squeeze over the rice.

# vegetables & salads

# potato & cheese gratin

## ingredients

### serves 4–6

900 g/2 lb waxy potatoes, peeled
    and thinly sliced
1 large garlic clove, halved
butter, for greasing and dotting
    over the top
225 ml/8 fl oz double cream
freshly grated nutmeg
salt and pepper
175 g/6 oz Gruyère cheese,
    finely grated

## method

1 Put the potato slices in a bowl, cover with cold water
and let stand for 5 minutes, then drain well.

2 Meanwhile, rub the bottom and sides of an oval
gratin or ovenproof dish with the cut sides of the garlic
halves, pressing down firmly to impart the flavour.
Lightly grease the sides of the dish with butter.

3 Place the potatoes in a bowl with the cream and
season with freshly grated nutmeg, salt and pepper.
Use your hands to mix everything together, then
transfer the potatoes to the gratin dish and pour over
any cream remaining in the bowl.

4 Sprinkle the cheese over the top and dot with butter.
Place the gratin dish on a baking sheet and bake in a
preheated oven, 190°C/375°F/Gas Mark 5, for 60–80
minutes, or until the potatoes are tender when pierced
with a skewer and the top is golden and bubbling. Let
stand for about 2 minutes, then serve straight from the
gratin dish.

# mushroom & cauliflower cheese crumble

## ingredients

### serves 4

1 medium cauliflower
55 g/2 oz butter
115 g/4 oz button mushrooms, sliced
salt and pepper

### for the topping

115 g/4 oz dry breadcrumbs
2 tbsp grated Parmesan cheese
1 tsp dried oregano
1 tsp dried parsley
2 tbsp butter

## method

1 Bring a large pan of salted water to the boil.

2 Break the cauliflower into small florets and cook in the boiling water for 3 minutes. Remove from the heat, drain well and transfer to a large shallow ovenproof dish.

3 Melt the butter in a small frying pan over a medium heat. Add the sliced mushrooms, stir to coat and cook gently for 3 minutes. Remove from the heat and add to the cauliflower. Season with salt and pepper.

4 Combine the breadcrumbs, cheese and herbs in a small mixing bowl, then sprinkle the crumbs over the vegetables.

5 Dice the butter for the topping and dot over the crumbs. Place the dish in a preheated oven, 230°C/450°F/Gas Mark 8, and bake for 15 minutes, or until the crumbs are golden brown and crisp. Serve from the cooking dish.

# leek & spinach pie

## ingredients
*serves 6–8*

225 g/8 oz puff pastry
2 tbsp unsalted butter
2 leeks, sliced finely
225 g/8 oz spinach, chopped
2 eggs
300 ml/10 fl oz double cream
pinch of dried thyme
salt and pepper

## method

1 Roll the pastry into a rectangle about 25 x 30 cm/
  10 x 12 inches. Leave to rest for 5 minutes, then press
  into a 20 x 25 cm/8 x 10 inch flan dish. Do not trim the
  overhang. Cover the pastry with aluminium foil
  and refrigerate.

2 Melt the butter in a large frying pan over a medium
  heat. Add the leeks, stir and cook gently for 5 minutes,
  or until soft. Add the spinach and cook for 3 minutes, c
  until soft. Leave to cool.

3 Beat the eggs in a bowl. Stir in the cream and season
  with thyme, salt and pepper. Remove the pastry case
  and uncover. Spread the cooked vegetables over the
  base. Pour in the egg mixture.

4 Place on a baking sheet and bake in a preheated oven,
  180°C/350°F/Gas Mark 4, for 30 minutes, or until set.
  Remove the flan from the oven and leave it to rest for
  10 minutes before serving.

# potato, fontina & rosemary tart

## ingredients

*serves 4*

1 quantity puff pastry
plain flour, for dusting

### filling

3–4 waxy potatoes
300 g/10½ oz Fontina cheese, cut into cubes
1 red onion, thinly sliced
3 large fresh rosemary sprigs
2 tbsp olive oil
salt and pepper
1 egg yolk

## method

1 Roll out the dough on a lightly floured counter into a circle about 25 cm/10 inches in diameter and put on a baking sheet.

2 Slice the potatoes as thinly as possible so that they are almost transparent – use a mandolin if you have one. Arrange the potato slices in a spiral, overlapping the slices to cover the pastry, leaving a 2-cm/³⁄₄-inch margin around the edge.

3 Arrange the cheese and onion over the potatoes, sprinkle with the rosemary and drizzle over the oil. Season to taste with salt and pepper and brush the edges with the egg yolk to glaze.

4 Bake in a preheated oven, 190°C/375°F/Gas Mark 5, for 25 minutes, or until the potatoes are tender and the pastry is brown and crisp. Serve hot.

# caramelized onion tart

## ingredients

### serves 4–6

100 g/3½ oz unsalted butter
600 g/1 lb 5 oz onions,
    thinly sliced
2 eggs
100 ml/3½ fl oz double cream
100 g/3½ oz grated Gruyère cheese
20-cm/8-inch baked pastry case
100 g/3½ oz grated Parmesan
    cheese
salt and pepper

## method

1 Melt the butter over a medium heat in a heavy frying
   pan. Stir in the onions and cook until they are well
   browned and caramelized. (This will take up to
   30 minutes, depending on the width of the pan.)
   Stir frequently to avoid burning. Remove the onions
   from the pan and set aside.

2 Beat the eggs in a large mixing bowl, stir in the cream
   and season with salt and pepper. Add the Gruyère and
   mix well. Mix in the cooked onions.

3 Pour the egg and onion mixture into the baked
   pastry case, sprinkle with Parmesan and place on an
   ovenproof tray. Bake in a preheated oven, 190°C/375°F,
   Gas Mark 5, for 15–20 minutes or until the filling has se
   and begun to brown.

4 Remove from the oven and leave to rest for at least
   10 minutes. The tart can be served hot or left to cool
   to room temperature.

# stuffed baked potatoes

## ingredients

### serves 4

900 g/2 lb baking potatoes,
    scrubbed
2 tbsp vegetable oil
1 tsp coarse sea salt
115 g/4 oz butter
1 small onion, chopped
salt and pepper
115 g/4 oz grated Cheddar cheese
    or crumbled Stilton cheese
snipped fresh chives,
    to garnish

### optional

4 tbsp canned, drained
    corn kernels
4 tbsp cooked mushrooms,
    courgettes or peppers

## method

1 Prick the potatoes in several places with a fork and put on a baking sheet. Brush with the oil and sprinkle with the salt. Bake in a preheated oven, 190°C/375°F/ Gas Mark 5, for 1 hour, or until the skins are crispy and the insides are soft when pierced with a fork.

2 Meanwhile, melt 1 tablespoon of the butter in a small frying pan over medium–low heat. Add the onion and cook, stirring occasionally, for 8–10 minutes until soft and golden. Set aside.

3 Cut the potatoes in half lengthways. Scoop the flesh into a large bowl, leaving the skins intact. Set aside the skins. Increase the oven temperature to 200°C/400°F/ Gas Mark 6.

4 Coarsely mash the potato flesh and mix in the onion and remaining butter. Add salt and pepper to taste and stir in any of the optional ingredients. Spoon the mixture back into the reserved potato skins. Top with the cheese.

5 Cook the filled potato skins in the oven for 10 minutes or until the cheese has melted and is beginning to brown. Garnish with chives and serve immediately.

# roasted ratatouille & potato wedges

## ingredients

### serves 4

300 g/10½ oz potatoes in their
   skins, scrubbed
200 g/7 oz aubergine,
   cut into wedges
125 g/4½ oz red onion,
   cut into slices
200 g/7 oz deseeded mixed
   peppers, sliced into strips
175 g/6 oz courgettes, cut in
   half lengthwise, then into slices
125 g/4½ oz cherry tomatoes
90 g/3¼ oz low-fat cream cheese
1 tsp runny honey
pinch of smoked paprika
1 tsp chopped fresh parsley

### marinade

1 tsp vegetable oil
1 tsp fresh rosemary
1 tbsp fresh lemon thyme
1 tbsp lemon juice
4 tbsp white wine
1 tsp sugar
2 tbsp chopped fresh basil
¼ tsp smoked paprika

## method

1 Bake the potatoes in a preheated oven, 200°C/400°F/
   Gas Mark 6, for 30 minutes, then remove and cut into
   wedges – the flesh should not be completely cooked.

2 To make the marinade, finely chop the rosemary and
   lemon thyme, then place all the ingredients in a bowl
   and blend with a hand-held electric blender until
   smooth, or use a food processor.

3 Put the potato wedges into a large bowl with the
   aubergine, onion, peppers and courgettes, then pour
   over the marinade and mix thoroughly.

4 Arrange the vegetables on a non-stick baking sheet
   and roast in the oven, turning occasionally, for 25–30
   minutes, or until golden brown and tender. Add the
   tomatoes for the last 5 minutes of the cooking time,
   just to split the skins and warm slightly.

5 Mix the cream cheese, honey and paprika together
   in a bowl.

6 Serve the vegetables with the cream cheese mixture
   and sprinkled with chopped parsley.

# vegetable chilli

## ingredients

### serves 4

1 aubergine, cut into
    2.5-cm/1-inch slices
1 tbsp olive oil, plus extra for
    brushing
1 large red onion, chopped finely
2 red or yellow peppers, deseeded
    and chopped finely
3–4 garlic cloves, finely chopped
    or crushed
800 g/1 lb 12 oz canned chopped
    tomatoes
1 tbsp mild chilli powder
½ tsp ground cumin
½ tsp dried oregano
2 small courgettes, quartered
    lengthways and sliced
400 g/14 oz canned kidney beans,
    drained and rinsed
450 ml/16 fl oz water
1 tbsp tomato purée
6 spring onions, chopped finely
115 g/4 oz Cheddar cheese, grated
salt and pepper

## method

1 Brush the aubergine slices on one side with olive oil.
Heat half the oil in a large, heavy-based frying pan
over a medium–high heat. Add the aubergine slices,
oiled-side up, and cook for 5–6 minutes, or until
browned on one side. Turn the slices over, cook on
the other side until browned and transfer to a plate.
Cut into bite-sized pieces.

2 Heat the remaining oil in a large saucepan over a
medium heat. Add the onion and peppers and cook,
stirring occasionally, for 3–4 minutes, or until the onion
is just softened, but not browned.

3 Add the garlic and cook for a further 2–3 minutes,
or until the onion is beginning to colour.

4 Add the tomatoes, chilli powder, cumin and oregano.
Season to taste with salt and pepper. Bring just to the
boil, reduce the heat, cover and simmer gently for
15 minutes.

5 Add the courgettes, aubergine pieces and kidney
beans. Stir in the water and the tomato purée. Return
to the boil, then cover and continue simmering for
45 minutes, or until the vegetables are tender. Taste
and adjust the seasoning if necessary. Ladle into
warmed serving bowls and top with spring onions
and cheese.

# cherry tomato clafoutis

## ingredients

### serves 4–6

400 g/14 oz cherry tomatoes

3 tbsp chopped fresh flat-leaf
　　parsley, snipped fresh chives,
　　or finely shredded fresh basil

100 g/3½ oz grated Gruyère cheese

55 g/2 oz plain flour

4 large eggs, lightly beaten

3 tbsp sour cream

225 ml/8 fl oz milk

salt and pepper

## method

1 Lightly grease an oval ovenproof dish. Arrange the
　cherry tomatoes in the dish and sprinkle with the herb
　and half the cheese.

2 Put the flour in a mixing bowl, then slowly add the
　eggs, whisking until smooth. Whisk in the sour cream,
　then slowly whisk in the milk to make a thin, smooth
　batter. Season with salt and pepper.

3 Gently pour the batter over the tomatoes, then sprinkl
　the top with the remaining cheese. Bake in a preheate
　oven, 190°C/375°F/Gas Mark 5, for 40–45 minutes,
　or until set and puffy, covering the top with foil if it
　browns too much before the batter sets. If serving hot,
　cool the clafoutis for a few minutes before cutting, or
　cool to room temperature.

# cheesy baked courgettes

## ingredients

### serves 4

4 medium courgettes
2 tbsp extra virgin olive oil
115 g/4 oz mozzarella cheese, sliced thinly
2 large tomatoes, deseeded and diced
2 tsp fresh basil or oregano, chopped

## method

*1* Slice the courgettes lengthways into 4 strips each. Brush with oil and place on an ovenproof tray.

*2* Bake the courgettes in a preheated oven, 200°C/400°F/ Gas Mark 6, for 10 minutes without letting them get too floppy.

*3* Remove the courgettes from the oven. Arrange slices of cheese on top and sprinkle with diced tomato and basil or oregano. Return to the oven for 5 minutes or until the cheese melts.

*4* Remove the courgettes from the oven and transfer carefully to serving plates, or serve straight from the baking dish.

# cheese & tomato pizza

## ingredients

### serves 4–6

23-cm/9-inch ready-made
thin-crust pizza base or
1 ciabatta loaf, sliced
horizontally
fresh basil leaves, torn

### for the tomato topping

150 ml/5 fl oz tomato passata
3 tbsp tomato purée
2 garlic cloves, crushed
pinch each of sugar, salt
and pepper
handful of cherry tomatoes

### for the cheese topping

150 ml/5 fl oz tomato passata
3 tbsp tomato purée
115 g/4 oz jar roasted peppers,
drained and thickly sliced
a few black olives
115 g/4 oz firm mozzarella
cheese, grated
55 g/2 oz Parmesan cheese, grated
salt and pepper

## method

1 To make the tomato topping, mix the passata, tomato
purée, garlic, sugar and salt and pepper together in a
bowl. Spread over the ready-made pizza base and
scatter with the cherry tomatoes.

2 To make the cheese topping, mix the tomato passata
and tomato purée together in a bowl and spread over
the pizza base. Top with the peppers and the olives.
Season with salt and pepper and scatter the mozzarella
and Parmesan cheeses over the top.

3 Bake in a preheated oven, 200°C/400°F/Gas Mark 6, for
8–10 minutes until hot and bubbling. Scatter with basil
leaves and serve immediately.

## variation

You can add different toppings to this basic tomato pizza
to create many variations, for example mushrooms and
pineapple for a tropical pizza or spicy chillies for a hot
pizza – the combinations are endless!

# broccoli & sesame frittata

## ingredients

### serves 2

175 g/6 oz broccoli, broken into
small florets
85 g/3 oz asparagus spears,
sliced diagonally
1 tbsp virgin olive oil
1 onion, cut into small wedges
2–4 garlic cloves, finely chopped
1 large orange pepper, deseeded
and chopped
4 eggs
3 tbsp cold water
salt and pepper
25 g/1 oz sesame seeds
15 g/¹/₂ oz freshly grated Parmesan
cheese
3 spring onions, finely sliced

## method

1 Cook the broccoli in a saucepan of lightly salted boiling
water for 4 minutes. Add the asparagus after 2 minutes.
Drain, then plunge into cold water. Drain again and
set aside.

2 Heat the oil in a large frying pan over low heat, add the
onion, garlic and orange pepper and cook, stirring
frequently, for 8 minutes, or until the vegetables have
softened.

3 Beat the eggs with the water, salt and pepper in a
medium-size bowl. Pour into the frying pan, add the
broccoli and asparagus and stir gently. Cook over
medium heat for 3–4 minutes, drawing the mixture
from the edges of the pan into the centre, allowing the
uncooked egg to flow to the edges of the pan. Preheat
the grill.

4 Sprinkle the top of the frittata with the sesame seeds
and cheese and cook under the preheated grill for
3–5 minutes, or until golden and set. Sprinkle with the
spring onions, cut into wedges and serve. Serve warm
or cold.

# courgette, carrot & tomato frittata

## ingredients

### serves 4

2 sprays olive oil
1 onion, cut into small wedges
1–2 garlic cloves, crushed
2 eggs
2 egg whites
1 courgette, about 85 g/3 oz,
    trimmed and grated
2 carrots, about 115 g/4 oz, peeled
    and grated
2 tomatoes, chopped
pepper
1 tbsp shredded fresh basil,
    for sprinkling

## method

1 Heat the oil in a large non-stick frying pan, add the onion and garlic and sauté for 5 minutes, stirring frequently. Beat the eggs and egg whites together in a bowl then pour into the pan. Using a spatula or fork, pull the egg mixture from the sides of the pan into the centre, allowing the uncooked egg to take its place.

2 Once the base has set lightly, add the grated courgette and carrots with the tomatoes. Add pepper to taste and continue to cook over a low heat until the eggs are set to personal preference.

3 Sprinkle with the shredded basil, cut the frittata into quarters and serve.

# mushroom stroganoff

## ingredients

### serves 4

550 g/1 lb 4 oz mixed fresh
    mushrooms, such as chestnut,
    chanterelles, cèpes and oyster
1 red onion, diced
2 garlic cloves, crushed
425 ml/15 fl oz vegetable stock
1 tbsp tomato paste
2 tbsp lemon juice
scant 1 tbsp cornflour
2 tbsp cold water
115 g/4 oz low-fat
    plain yogurt
3 tbsp chopped fresh parsley
pepper
boiled brown or white rice and
    crisp green salad, to serve

## method

1 Put the mushrooms, onion, garlic, stock, tomato paste
    and lemon juice into a saucepan and bring to the boil.
    Reduce the heat, cover and simmer for 15 minutes, or
    until the onion is tender.

2 Blend the cornflour with the water in a small bowl and
    stir into the mushroom mixture. Return to the boil,
    stirring constantly, and cook until the sauce thickens.
    Reduce the heat and simmer for a further 2–3 minutes,
    stirring occasionally.

3 Just before serving, remove the pan from the heat,
    and stir in the yogurt, making sure that the stroganoff
    is not boiling or it may separate and curdle. Stir in
    2 tablespoons of the parsley and season with pepper.
    Transfer the stroganoff to a warmed serving dish,
    sprinkle over the remaining parsley and serve at once
    with boiled brown or white rice and a crisp green salad.

# thai yellow vegetable curry with brown basmati rice

## ingredients

### serves 4

50 g/1¾ oz yellow pepper
50 g/1¾ oz celery
50 g/1¾ oz baby corn
85 g/3 oz leek
100 g/3½ oz sweet potato
100 g/3½ oz pak choi
50 g/1¾ oz courgette
50 g/1¾ oz mangetout
300 ml/10 fl oz pineapple juice
200 ml/7 fl oz water
3 tbsp lime juice
2 tbsp cornflour
4 tbsp low-fat plain yogurt
4 tbsp chopped fresh coriander
150 g/5½ oz cooked brown
   basmati rice

### spice mix

1 tsp finely chopped garlic
¼ tsp ground turmeric
1 tsp ground coriander
1 tsp finely chopped lemongrass
3 kaffir lime leaves
1 tsp finely chopped green chilli

## method

1 To make the spice mix, pound all the spices to a fine paste using a mortar and pestle.

2 To prepare the vegetables, cut the yellow pepper into 1-cm/½-inch squares, cut the celery, baby corn and leek into 5-mm/¼-inch lengths, and cut the sweet potato into 1-cm/ ½-inch cubes. Shred the pak choi. Cut the courgette into 5-mm/¼-inch cubes and slice the mangetout into thin strips.

3 Put the pepper, celery, baby corn, leek, sweet potato, pineapple juice, water and the spice mix into a large saucepan with a lid and bring to the boil. Reduce the heat and skim the scum from the surface with a metal spoon. Cover and simmer for 15 minutes.

4 Add the pak choi, courgette and mangetout and cook for 2 minutes. Add the lime juice, then gradually add the cornflour blended with a little cold water. Cook, stirring constantly, until thickened to the required consistency.

5 Remove the curry from the heat and cool for 2–3 minutes. Stir in the yogurt. (Do not boil once the yogurt has been added or the curry will separate.) Stir in the fresh coriander and serve the curry with the rice

# roasted garlic mashed potatoes

## ingredients

*serves 4*

2 whole garlic bulbs
1 tbsp olive oil
900 g/2 lb floury potatoes, peeled
125 ml/4 fl oz milk
55 g/2 oz butter
salt and pepper

## method

1 Separate the garlic cloves, place on a large piece of foil and drizzle with the oil. Wrap the garlic in the foil and roast in a preheated oven, 180°C/350°F/Gas Mark 4, for about 1 hour, or until very tender. Let cool slightly.

2 Meanwhile, cut the potatoes into chunks, then cook in a saucepan of lightly salted boiling water for 15 minutes, or until tender.

3 Squeeze the cooled garlic cloves out of their skins and push through a sieve into a saucepan. Add the milk and butter and season with salt and pepper. Heat gently until the butter has melted.

4 Drain the cooked potatoes, then mash in the pan until smooth. Pour in the garlic mixture and heat gently, stirring, until the ingredients are combined. Serve hot.

# roasted squash wedges

## ingredients

### serves 4

200 g/7 oz butternut squash
   or other type of squash,
   peeled, deseeded and
   cut into 4 wedges
1 tsp vegetable oil
100 g/3½ oz onion,
   finely chopped
1 tsp minced garlic
70 g/2½ oz three-grain risotto mix
   (baldo rice, spelt and pearl
   barley – this is available
   ready-mixed)
300 ml/10 fl oz vegetable stock
225 g/8 oz asparagus tips
2 tbsp finely chopped fresh
   marjoram, plus extra
   to garnish
3 tbsp low-fat cream cheese
2 tbsp finely chopped
   fresh parsley
pepper

## method

1 Spread out the squash wedges on a non-stick baking sheet and roast in a preheated oven, 200°C/400°F/Gas Mark 6, for 20 minutes, or until the wedges are tender and golden brown.

2 Meanwhile, heat the oil in a medium saucepan over high heat, add the onion and garlic and cook, stirring, until softened but not coloured. Add the risotto mix and stir in half the stock. Simmer, stirring occasionally, until the stock has reduced in the pan. Pour in the remaining stock and continue to cook, stirring occasionally, until the grains are tender.

3 Cut 175 g/6 oz of the asparagus into 10-cm/4-inch lengths and blanch in a saucepan of boiling water for 2 minutes. Drain and keep warm. Cut the remaining asparagus into 5-mm/¼-inch slices and add to the risotto for the last 3 minutes of the cooking time.

4 Remove the risotto from the heat and stir in the marjoram, cream cheese and parsley. Season with pepper. Do not reboil.

5 To serve, lay the squash wedges on warmed serving plates, then spoon over the risotto and top with the asparagus. Garnish with marjoram.

# colcannon

## ingredients

### serves 4

225 g/8 oz green cabbage, shredded
5 tbsp milk
225 g/8 oz floury potatoes, diced
1 large leek, chopped
pinch of freshly grated nutmeg
1 tbsp butter, melted
salt and pepper

## method

1 Cook the shredded cabbage in a saucepan of boiling salted water for 7–10 minutes. Drain thoroughly and set aside.

2 Meanwhile, in a separate saucepan, bring the milk to the boil and add the potatoes and leek. Reduce the heat and simmer for 15–20 minutes, or until they are cooked through.

3 Remove from the heat, stir in the freshly grated nutmeg and thoroughly mash the potatoes and leek together.

4 Add the drained cabbage to the mashed potato and leek mixture, season to taste and mix together well.

5 Spoon the mixture into a warmed serving dish, making a hollow in the centre with the back of a spoon.

6 Pour the melted butter into the hollow and serve the colcannon at once, while it is still hot.

# stir-fried broccoli

## ingredients

### serves 4

2 tbsp vegetable oil
2 broccoli heads,
    cut into florets
2 tbsp soy sauce
1 tsp cornflour
1 tbsp caster sugar
1 tsp grated fresh ginger
1 garlic clove, crushed
pinch of dried red pepper flakes
1 tsp toasted sesame seeds,
    to garnish

## method

1 Heat the oil in a large preheated wok or frying pan over high heat until almost smoking. Add the broccoli and stir-fry for 4–5 minutes. Reduce the heat to medium.

2 Combine the soy sauce, cornflour, sugar, ginger, garlic and red pepper flakes in a small bowl. Add the mixture to the broccoli and cook, stirring constantly, for 2–3 minutes until the sauce thickens slightly.

3 Transfer to a warmed serving dish, garnish with the sesame seeds and serve immediately.

# roasted onions

## ingredients

*serves 4*

8 large onions, peeled
3 tbsp olive oil
55 g/2 oz butter
2 tsp chopped fresh thyme
salt and pepper
200 g/7 oz Cheddar cheese, grated

## method

1 Cut a cross down through the top of the onions towards the root, without cutting all the way through. Place the onions in a roasting pan and drizzle over the olive oil.

2 Press a little of the butter into the open crosses, sprinkle with the thyme and season with salt and pepper. Cover with foil and roast in a preheated oven, 180°C/350°F/ Gas Mark 4, for 40–45 minutes.

3 Remove from the oven, take off the foil and baste the onions with the pan juices. Return to the oven and cook for a further 15 minutes, uncovered, to allow the onions to brown.

4 Take the onions out of the oven and scatter the grated cheese over them. Return them to the oven for a few minutes so that the cheese starts to melt. Serve immediately.

# brussels sprouts with chestnuts

## ingredients

### serves 4

450 g/1 lb Brussels sprouts
115 g/4 oz unsalted butter
55 g/2 oz brown sugar
115 g/4 oz cooked and peeled
    chestnuts

## method

1 Trim the Brussels sprouts and remove and discard any loose outer leaves. Add to a large saucepan of boiling salted water and boil for 5–10 minutes until just tender, but not too soft. Drain well, refresh under cold water and drain again. Set aside.

2 Melt the butter in a heavy-based frying pan over medium heat. Add the sugar and stir until dissolved. Add the chestnuts and cook, stirring occasionally, until well coated and beginning to brown.

3 Add the sprouts to the chestnuts and mix well. Reduce the heat and cook gently, stirring occasionally, for 3–4 minutes to heat through.

4 Remove from the heat, transfer to a warmed serving dish and serve immediately.

# tabbouleh

## ingredients

*serves 4*

175 g/6 oz bulgur wheat
3 tbsp extra-virgin olive oil
4 tbsp lemon juice
salt and pepper
4 spring onions
1 green pepper, deseeded
    and sliced
4 tomatoes, chopped
2 tbsp chopped fresh parsley
2 tbsp chopped fresh mint
8 black olives, pitted

## method

1 Place the bulgur wheat in a large bowl and add enoug
   cold water to cover. Let stand for 30 minutes, or until
   the wheat has doubled in size. Drain well and press ou
   as much liquid as possible. Spread out the wheat on
   paper towels to dry.

2 Place the wheat in a serving bowl. Mix the olive oil and
   lemon juice together in a jug and season to taste with
   salt and pepper. Pour the lemon mixture over the
   wheat and marinate for 1 hour.

3 Using a sharp knife, finely chop the spring onions,
   then add to the salad with the green pepper, tomatoes,
   parsley and mint and toss lightly to mix. Top the salad
   with the olives and serve immediately.

# greek salad

## ingredients

### serves 4

4 tomatoes, cut into wedges
1 onion, sliced
½ cucumber, sliced
225 g/8 oz kalamata olives, stoned
225 g/8 oz Feta cheese, cubed
2 tbsp fresh coriander leaves
fresh flat-leaf parsley sprigs,
    to garnish
pitta bread, to serve

### dressing

5 tbsp extra-virgin olive oil
2 tbsp white wine vinegar
1 tbsp lemon juice
½ tsp sugar
1 tbsp chopped fresh coriander
salt and pepper

## method

1 To make the dressing, put all the ingredients for the
  dressing into a large bowl and mix well together.

2 Add the tomatoes, onion, cucumber, olives, cheese and
  coriander. Toss all the ingredients together, then divide
  between individual serving bowls. Garnish with parsley
  sprigs and serve with pitta bread.

# roasted pepper salad

## ingredients

### serves 8

3 red peppers
3 yellow peppers
5 tbsp Spanish extra-virgin olive oil
2 tbsp dry sherry vinegar or lemon
    juice
2 garlic cloves, crushed
pinch of sugar
salt and pepper
1 tbsp capers
8 small black Spanish olives
2 tbsp chopped fresh marjoram,
    plus extra sprigs to garnish

## method

1 Preheat the grill to high. Place the peppers on a wire rack or grill pan and cook under the grill for 10 minutes until their skins have blackened and blistered, turning them frequently.

2 Remove the roasted peppers from the heat, and either put them in a bowl and immediately cover tightly with a clean, damp tea towel or put them in a plastic bag. The steam helps to soften the skins and makes it easier to remove them. Let stand for about 15 minutes, until cool enough to handle.

3 Holding one pepper at a time over a clean bowl, use a sharp knife to make a small hole in the base and gently squeeze out the juices and reserve them. Still holding the pepper over the bowl, carefully peel off the blackened skin with your fingers, or a knife, and discard it. Cut the peppers in half and remove the stem, core and seeds, then cut each pepper into neat thin strips. Arrange the pepper strips on a serving dish.

4 To the reserved pepper juices add the olive oil, sherry vinegar, garlic, sugar, salt and pepper. Whisk until combined. Drizzle the dressing evenly over the salad.

5 Sprinkle the capers, olives and chopped marjoram over the salad, garnish with marjoram sprigs and serve at room temperature.

# moroccan tomato & red pepper salad

## ingredients

*serves 4*

3 red peppers
4 ripe tomatoes
½ bunch of fresh
    coriander, chopped
2 garlic cloves, finely chopped
salt and pepper

## method

1 Preheat the grill. Place the peppers on a baking sheet and cook under the grill, turning occasionally, for 15 minutes. Add the tomatoes and grill, turning occasionally, for a further 5–10 minutes, or until all the skins are charred and blistered. Remove from the heat and leave to cool.

2 Peel and deseed the peppers and tomatoes and slice the flesh thinly. Place in a bowl, mix well and season with salt and pepper. Sprinkle with the coriander and garlic, cover with clingfilm and chill in the refrigerator for at least 1 hour. Just before serving, drain off any excess liquid.

# green bean salad with feta cheese

## ingredients

### serves 4

350 g/12 oz green beans
1 red onion, chopped
3–4 tbsp chopped fresh coriander
2 radishes, thinly sliced
75 g/2³/₄ oz Feta cheese drained
    weight, crumbled
1 tsp chopped fresh oregano,
    plus extra leaves to garnish
    (optional), or ¹/₂ tsp dried
    oregano
pepper
2 tbsp red wine or fruit vinegar
80 ml/3 fl oz extra-virgin olive oil
3 ripe tomatoes, cut into wedges
slices of crusty bread,
    to serve

## method

1 Bring about 5 cm/2 inches of water to the boil in the bottom of a steamer. Add the beans to the top part of the steamer, cover and steam for 5 minutes, or until just tender.

2 Place the beans in a large bowl and add the onion, coriander, radishes and Feta cheese.

3 Sprinkle the oregano over the salad, then season with pepper. Mix the vinegar and oil together in a small bowl and pour over the salad. Toss gently to mix well.

4 Transfer to a serving platter, surround with the tomato wedges and serve at once with slices of crusty bread, or cover and chill until ready to serve.

# nutty beetroot salad

## ingredients

### serves 4

3 tbsp red wine vinegar
   or fruit vinegar
3 cooked beetroot, grated
2 tart apples, eg Granny Smith
2 tbsp lemon juice
4 large handfuls mixed salad leaves
4 tbsp pecans

### for the dressing

50 ml/2 fl oz plain yoghurt
50 ml/2 fl oz mayonnaise
1 garlic clove, chopped
1 tbsp chopped fresh dill
salt and pepper

## method

1 Sprinkle vinegar over the beetroot, cover with clingfilm and chill for at least 4 hours.

2 Core and slice the apples, place the slices in a dish and sprinkle with the lemon juice.

3 Combine the dressing ingredients in a small bowl. Remove the beetroot from the refrigerator and dress. Add the apples to the beetroot and mix gently to coat with the salad dressing.

4 To serve, arrange a handful of salad leaves on each plate and top with a large spoonful of the apple and beetroot mixture.

5 Toast the pecans in a dry frying pan over a medium heat for 2 minutes, or until they begin to brown. Sprinkle over the beetroot and apple to garnish.

# warm goat's cheese mixed leaf salad

## ingredients

*serves 4*

1 small iceberg lettuce,
    torn into pieces
handful of rocket leaves
few radicchio leaves, torn
6 slices French bread
115 g/4 oz goat's cheese, sliced

**for the dressing**
4 tbsp extra virgin olive oil
1 tbsp white wine vinegar
salt and pepper

## method

1 Preheat the grill. Divide all the leaves between 4 individual salad bowls.

2 Toast one side of the bread under the grill until golden. Place a slice of cheese on top of each untoasted side and toast until the cheese is just melting.

3 Put all the dressing ingredients into a bowl and beat together until combined. Pour over the leaves, tossing to coat.

4 Cut each slice of bread in half and place 3 halves on top of each salad. Toss very gently to combine and serve warm.

# red onion, tomato & herb salad

## ingredients

### serves 4

900 g/2 lb tomatoes, sliced thinly
1 tbsp sugar (optional)
1 red onion, sliced thinly
large handful coarsely chopped
    fresh herbs
salt and pepper

### for the dressing

2–4 tbsp vegetable oil
2 tbsp red wine vinegar or fruit
    vinegar

## method

1 Arrange the tomato slices in a shallow bowl. Sprinkle with sugar (if using), salt and pepper.

2 Separate the onion slices into rings and scatter over the tomatoes. Sprinkle the herbs over the top. Anything that is in season can be used – for example, tarragon, sorrel, coriander or basil.

3 Place the dressing ingredients in a jar with a screw-top lid. Shake well. Pour the dressing over the salad and mix gently.

4 Cover with clingfilm and refrigerate for 20 minutes. Remove the salad from the refrigerator 5 minutes before serving, unwrap the dish and stir gently before setting out on the table.

# desserts

# rich vanilla ice cream

## ingredients

*serves 4–6*

300 ml/10 fl oz single cream and 300 ml/10 fl oz double cream or 625ml/20 fl oz whipping cream
1 vanilla bean
4 large egg yolks
100 g/3½ oz caster sugar

## method

1 Pour the single and double cream or whipping cream into a large heavy-based saucepan. Split open the vanilla bean and scrape out the seeds into the cream, then add the whole vanilla bean too. Bring almost to the boil, then remove from the heat and infuse for 30 minutes.

2 Put the egg yolks and sugar in a large bowl and whisk together until pale and the mixture leaves a trail when the whisk is lifted. Remove the vanilla bean from the cream, then slowly add the cream to the egg mixture, stirring all the time with a wooden spoon. Strain the mixture into the rinsed-out pan or a double boiler and cook over low heat for 10–15 minutes, stirring all the time, until the mixture thickens enough to coat the back of the spoon. Do not let the mixture boil or it will curdle. Remove the custard from the heat and cool for at least 1 hour, stirring from time to time to prevent a skin forming.

3 Churn the custard in an ice-cream maker following the manufacturer's instructions. Serve immediately if wished, or transfer to a freezerproof container, cover with a lid and store in the freezer.

# lemon yogurt ice cream

## ingredients

### serves 4–6

2–3 lemons
625 ml/20 fl oz Greek-style yogurt
150 ml/5 fl oz double cream
100 g/3½ oz caster sugar
finely pared orange rind,
      to garnish

## method

1 Squeeze the juice from the lemons – you need
   6 tablespoons in total. Put the juice into a bowl, add
   the yogurt, cream and sugar, and mix well together.

2 If using an ice-cream machine, churn the mixture in
   the machine following the manufacturer's instructions.
   Alternatively, freeze the mixture in a freezerproof
   container, uncovered, for 1–2 hours, or until it starts to
   set around the edges.

3 Turn the mixture into a bowl and stir with a fork or beat
   in a food processor until smooth. Return to the freezer
   and freeze for a further 2–3 hours, or until firm or
   required. Cover the container with a lid for storing.
   Serve with finely pared orange rind.

# raspberry ripple ice cream

## ingredients

*serves 6*

85 g/3 oz fresh or frozen
    raspberries, thawed if frozen,
    plus extra to serve
2 tbsp water
2 eggs
1 tbsp caster sugar
300 ml/10 fl oz milk, warmed
1 tsp vanilla essence
300 ml/10 fl oz double cream

## method

*1* Turn the freezer to rapid. Put the raspberries into a
saucepan with the water and bring to the boil, then
reduce the heat and simmer gently for 5 minutes.
Remove from the heat and cool for 30 minutes. Transfer
to a food processor or blender and process to a purée,
then rub through a nylon sieve to remove the pips.
Set aside.

*2* Beat the eggs in a bowl. Stir the sugar into the
warmed milk, then slowly pour onto the eggs, beating
constantly. Strain into a clean saucepan and cook over
low heat, stirring constantly, for 8–10 minutes, or
until the custard thickens and coats the back of a
wooden spoon. Add the vanilla essence, remove from
the heat and let cool.

*3* Half-whip the cream in a large bowl, then slowly stir in
the cooled custard. Pour into a freezerproof container
and freeze for up to 2 hours, or until starting to set
around the outside. Remove from the freezer and stir
the mixture, breaking up any ice crystals.

*4* Return the mixture to the freezer and freeze for a
further hour, then remove from the freezer again and
gently stir in the raspberry purée to give a rippled
effect. Return to the freezer for a further hour or until
frozen. Serve in scoops with extra fresh raspberries.

# icy fruit blizzard

## ingredients

*serves 4*

1 pineapple

1 large piece seeded watermelon, peeled and cut into small pieces

225 g/8 oz strawberries or other berries, hulled and left whole or sliced

1 mango, peach or nectarine, peeled and sliced

1 banana, peeled and sliced

orange juice

caster sugar, to taste

## method

1 Cover 2 non-stick baking sheets or ordinary baking sheets with a sheet of clingfilm. Arrange the fruits on top and open freeze for at least 2 hours, or until firm and icy.

2 Place one type of fruit in a food processor and process until it is all broken up into small pieces.

3 Add a little orange juice and sugar to taste, and continue to process until it forms a granular mixture. Repeat with the remaining fruits. Arrange in chilled bowls and serve immediately.

# blueberry frozen yogurt

## ingredients

*serves 4*

175 g/6 oz fresh blueberries
finely grated rind and
    juice of 1 orange
3 tbsp maple syrup
500 g/1 lb 2 oz plain
    low-fat yogurt

## method

1 Put the blueberries and orange juice into a food processor or blender and process to a purée. Strain through a nylon sieve into a bowl or jug.

2 Stir the maple syrup and yogurt together in a large mixing bowl, then fold in the fruit purée.

3 Churn the mixture in an ice-cream machine, following the manufacturer's instructions, then freeze for 5–6 hours. If you don't have an ice-cream machine, transfer the mixture to a freezerproof container, and freeze for 2 hours. Remove from the freezer, turn out into a bowl and beat until smooth. Return to the freezer and freeze until firm.

# apricot & passion fruit sorbet

## ingredients

*serves 6*

### sorbet

100 g/3½ oz no-soak dried apricots
250 ml/9 fl oz water
2 tbsp freshly squeezed
 lemon juice
2 tbsp freshly squeezed
 orange juice
7 tbsp passion fruit pulp, sieved
 to remove the seeds

### sesame snaps

1 tbsp sesame seeds
1 tbsp liquid glucose
3 tbsp caster sugar
2 tbsp plain flour

## method

1 To make the sorbet, put the apricots in a saucepan with the water and bring to the boil. Reduce the heat and simmer for 10–15 minutes, or until soft. Remove from the heat. Purée the apricots in a food processor with the water, then blend in the lemon juice, orange juice and 3 tablespoons of the passion fruit pulp.

2 Add 2 tablespoons of the passion fruit pulp, mix well, then transfer to a large, freezerproof container and freeze for 20 minutes. Beat the sorbet to break down the ice crystals, then return to the freezer for a further 2 hours, or until fully frozen, beating every 20 minutes to give a smooth texture to the finished sorbet.

3 To make the sesame snaps, toss the sesame seeds in a small saucepan over high heat until golden brown. Remove from the heat, add the glucose, sugar and flour and mix with a metal spoon to form a sticky paste. Remove from the pan and cool slightly. Roll the paste into a sausage shape and cut into 16 pieces. With wet hands, roll each piece into a small ball, then lightly press out onto a sheet of silicone.

4 Bake in a preheated oven, 180°C/350°F/Gas Mark 4, for 6 minutes until golden. Transfer to a wire rack and let cool. Serve the sorbet with the remaining passion fruit pulp spooned over, along with the sesame snaps.

# spanish caramel custard

## ingredients

### serves 6

500 ml/18 fl oz whole milk
½ orange with 2 long, thin pieces
   of rind pared off and reserved
1 vanilla bean, split, or
   ½ tsp vanilla essence
175 g/6 oz caster sugar
butter, for greasing the dish
3 large eggs, plus 2 large
   egg yolks

## method

1 Pour the milk into a saucepan with the orange rind and vanilla bean or essence. Bring to the boil, then remove from the heat and stir in 85 g/3 oz of the sugar; set aside for at least 30 minutes to infuse.

2 Meanwhile, put the remaining sugar and 4 tablespoons of water in another saucepan over medium–high heat. Stir until the sugar dissolves, then boil without stirring until the caramel turns deep golden brown. Remove from the heat at once and squeeze in a few drops of orange juice. Pour into a lightly buttered 1-litre/32-fl oz soufflé dish and swirl to cover the base; set aside.

3 Return the pan of infused milk to the heat, and bring to a simmer. Beat the whole eggs and egg yolks together in a heatproof bowl. Pour the warm milk into the eggs, whisking constantly. Strain into the soufflé dish.

4 Place the soufflé dish in a roasting pan and pour in enough boiling water to come halfway up the sides of the dish. Bake in a preheated oven, 160°C/325°F/Gas Mark 2½, for 75–90 minutes until set and a knife inserted in the centre comes out clean. Remove the dish from the roasting pan, set aside to cool, then cover and chill overnight. To serve, run a metal spatula round the dish, then invert onto a serving plate, shaking firmly to release.

# creamy mango brûlée

## ingredients

*serves 4*

2 mangoes
250 g/9 oz Mascarpone cheese
200 ml/7 fl oz Greek-style yogurt
1 tsp ground ginger
grated rind and juice of 1 lime
2 tbsp soft light brown sugar
8 tbsp raw brown sugar

## method

1 Slice the mangoes on either side of the stone. Discard the stone and peel the fruit. Slice and then chop the fruit. Divide it between 4 ramekins.

2 Beat the Mascarpone cheese with the yogurt. Fold in the ginger, lime rind and juice and soft brown sugar. Divide the mixture between the ramekins and level off the tops. Chill for 2 hours.

3 Sprinkle 2 tablespoons of raw brown sugar over the top of each dish, covering the creamy mixture. Place under a hot grill for 2–3 minutes, until melted and browned. Let cool, then chill until needed. This dessert should be eaten on the day it is made.

# mascarpone creams

## ingredients

*Serves 4*

115 g/4 oz Amaretti biscuits, crushed
4 tbsp Amaretto or Maraschino
4 eggs, separated
55 g/2 oz caster sugar
225 g/8 oz Mascarpone cheese
toasted flaked almonds, to decorate

## method

1 Place the Amaretti crumbs in a bowl, add the Amaretto or Maraschino and set aside to soak.

2 Meanwhile, beat the egg yolks with the caster sugar until pale and thick. Fold in the Mascarpone and soaked biscuit crumbs.

3 Whisk the egg whites in a separate, spotlessly clean bowl until stiff, then gently fold into the cheese mixture. Divide the Mascarpone cream between 4 serving dishes and chill for 1–2 hours. Sprinkle with toasted slivered almonds just before serving.

# creamy chocolate pudding

## ingredients

### serves 4–6

175 g/6 oz plain chocolate, at least
70% cocoa solids, broken up
1½ tbsp orange juice
3 tbsp water
2 tbsp unsalted butter, diced
2 eggs, seaparated
⅛ tsp cream of tartar
3 tbsp caster sugar
6 tbsp double cream
orange wedges, to serve

### pistachio-orange
praline

corn oil, for greasing
55 g/2 oz caster sugar
55 g/2 oz shelled pistachios
finely grated rind of
1 large orange

## method

1 Melt the chocolate with the orange juice and water in
a small saucepan over very low heat, stirring constantly.
Remove from the heat and melt in the butter until
incorporated. Scrape the chocolate into a bowl. Beat
the egg yolks until blended, then beat them into the
chocolate mixture. Set aside to cool.

2 In a bowl, whisk the egg whites with the cream of
tartar until soft peaks form. Beat in 1 tablespoon of the
sugar, at a time, beating well after each addition, until
the meringue is glossy. Beat 1 tablespoon of the
meringue into the chocolate, then fold in the rest.

3 In a separate bowl, whip the cream until soft peaks
form. Fold into the chocolate mixture. Spoon into
individual glass bowls or wine glasses or 1 large serving
bowl. Cover with clingfilm and chill for at least 4 hours.

4 To make the praline, lightly grease a baking sheet with
corn oil and set aside. Put the sugar and pistachios in
a small saucepan over medium heat. When the sugar
starts to melt, stir gently until a liquid caramel forms
and the nuts start popping. Pour the praline onto the
baking sheet and immediately finely grate the orange
rind over. Cool until firm then coarsely chop. Just
before serving, sprinkle the praline over the chocolate
pudding and serve with orange wedges.

# summer pudding

## ingredients

### serves 6

675 g/1 lb 8 oz mixed soft fruits,
    such as redcurrants,
    blackcurrants, raspberries
    and blackberries
140 g/5 oz caster sugar
2 tbsp crème de framboise liqueur
    (optional)
6–8 slices of good day-old white
    bread, crusts removed
double cream, to serve

## method

1 Place the fruits in a large saucepan with the sugar. Over low heat, very slowly bring to the boil, stirring carefully to ensure that the sugar has dissolved. Cook over low heat for only 2–3 minutes, until the juices run but the fruit still holds its shape. Add the liqueur if using.

2 Line an 875-ml/28-fl oz pudding bowl with some of the slices of bread (cut them to shape so that the bread fits well). Spoon in the cooked fruit and juices, reserving a little of the juice for later.

3 Cover the surface of the fruit with the remaining bread. Place a plate on top of the pudding and weight it down for at least 8 hours or overnight in the refrigerator.

4 Turn out the pudding and pour over the reserved juices to colour any white bits of bread that may still be showing. Serve with the double cream.

# baked apricots with honey

## ingredients

*serves 4*

butter, for greasing
4 apricots, each cut in half
    and pitted
4 tbsp flaked almonds
4 tbsp honey
pinch ground ginger or grated
    nutmeg

## method

1 Lightly butter an ovenproof dish large enough to hold the apricot halves in a single layer.

2 Arrange the apricot halves in the dish, cut side up. Sprinkle with the almonds and drizzle the honey over. Dust with the spice.

3 Bake in a preheated oven, 200°C/400°F/Gas Mark 6, for 12–15 minutes until the apricots are tender and the almonds golden. Remove from the oven and serve at once.

# banoffee pies

## ingredients

### serves 4

two cans sweetened condensed
     milk, about 400 ml/
     14 fl oz each
6 tbsp butter, melted
150 g/5½ oz digestive biscuits,
     crushed into crumbs
50 g/1¾ oz almonds, toasted
     and ground
50 g/1¾ oz hazelnuts, toasted
     and ground
4 ripe bananas
1 tbsp lemon juice
1 tsp vanilla essence
75 g/2¾ oz chocolate flakes
450 ml/16 fl oz thick double
     cream, whipped

## method

1 Place the cans of milk in a large saucepan and cover
   them with water. Bring to the boil, then reduce the heat
   and simmer for 2 hours, topping up the water level
   regularly to keep the cans covered. Carefully lift out the
   hot cans and set aside to cool.

2 Grease 4 individual loose-based tartlet pans with butter.
   Put the remaining butter into a bowl and add the
   biscuit crumbs and nuts. Mix together well, then press
   the mixture evenly into the bottom of the tartlet pans.
   Bake in a preheated oven, 180°C/350°F/Gas Mark 4, for
   10–12 minutes, then remove from the oven and cool.

3 Open the cans of condensed milk and spread the
   contents over the biscuit base in the tartlet pans.
   Peel and slice the bananas and put them into a bowl.
   Sprinkle over the lemon juice and vanilla essence
   and mix gently. Spoon the banana mixture onto the
   condensed milk layer, then top with a dollop of
   whipped cream. Break up the chocolate flakes, scatter
   over the tartlets and serve.

# blueberry filo tart

## ingredients

*serves 2*

4 sheets of filo pastry
rapeseed or vegetable oil spray
200 g/7 oz Mascarpone cheese
1 tsp honey
1 tbsp finely grated
    lemon rind
3 tbsp lemon juice
1 tsp caster sugar
100 g/3½ oz fresh blueberries

## method

*1* Using a plate as a guide, cut out 4 x 14-cm/5½-inch circles of filo pastry (you need two circles per tartlet). Spray each lightly with oil before laying two circles into 2 x 10-cm/4-inch fluted tartlet pans, pressing the pastry into the corners. Prick the bases with a fork.

*2* Put a ramekin into the centre of each tartlet shell to prevent the pastry rising, then bake in a preheated oven, 180°C/350°F/Gas Mark 4, for 5 minutes. Remove the ramekins and bake the cases for a further 4–5 minutes so that the bases cook. Remove from the oven and leave the shells to cool in the tins. Store in an airtight tin so that they remain crisp.

*3* Mix the Mascarpone cheese with the honey in a small bowl.

*4* Put the lemon rind and juice and the sugar in a small saucepan over low heat and heat until the liquid has evaporated, then add the blueberries. Stir with a metal spoon to coat the berries in the syrup. Remove from the heat and keep warm.

*5* To serve, place each tartlet shell on a serving plate, add a spoonful of the Mascarpone mixture, then spoon over the warmed blueberries.

# index